ORDER
IN THE
COURT

REFLECTIONS ON THE ESSENCE OF THE LAW

ORDER IN THE COURT

Crafting a More Just World in Lawless Times

Benjamin Sells

ELEMENT

Boston, Massachusetts • Shaftesbury, Dorset
Melbourne, Victoria

Published in the USA in 1999 by
Element Books, Inc.
160 North Washington Street
Boston, MA 02114

Published in Great Britain in 1999 by
Element Books Limited
Shaftesbury, Dorset SP7 8BP

Published in Australia in 1999 by
Element Books Limited for
Penguin Australia Limited
487 Maroondah Highway, Ringwood, Victoria 3134

Library of Congress Cataloging-in-Publication Data

Sells, Benjamin.
Order in the court : crafting a more just world in lawless times / Benjamin Sells.
p. cm.
ISBN 1-86204-443-0
1. Natural law. 2. Law and ethics. 3. Law — Psychological aspects. 4. Culture and law. I. Title.
K474.S45O73 1999
340.112--dc21 98-031402
CIP

Printed and bound in the United States by Edwards Brothers

Contents

Acknowledgments

THE BOOK you hold in your hands would not exist without the kind and generous support of many people. In particular, I thank Charles Carman and Bruce Rubenstein of *Illinois Legal Times,* who first encouraged me to write on the subject of the soul of the law and who have given a home to my work for many years. I also thank my teachers and friends James Hillman and Thomas Moore, whose ideas and inspiration are present on every page of this book. And I thank my wife, Rima Cepenas, whose beauty and fullness of soul remind me daily of the eternal connection between the two.

Introduction

WE LIVE in a time when the Law has become countercultural. And because the Law inspires the soul of each of us, when the Law suffers in isolation from culture we will reflect its pain and anger.

At first blush, to claim the Law countercultural seems incredible. Building prisons has become a growth industry. Each year the volumes of laws, rules, and regulations promulgated by our lawmakers grow thicker and more intrusive. Lawsuits continue to skyrocket as citizens replace discourse with depositions and leaders set aside debate and compromise in favor of litigation and subpoenas. Everywhere, people lay claim to individual rights defined to a scalpel's edge, leaving us all edgy with thin skins easier and easier to cut. Humor becomes a slight, a showing of simple interest converts to harassment, and talk of justice falls mute before the shouts and accusations of adjudication. Even the health of our people now falls under the rubric of management and bureaucratic control.

But to my mind the proliferation of laws, our too-quick resort to the legal system, and the ever-burgeoning systems of bureaucracy that dominate modern life are all evidence that we live in a time of increasing lawlessness. Only when things lose their intrinsic value must we have more and more of them, and so only as the Law diminishes in our souls do we try to replace it with rules and systems, much like a people who reject the Gods must erect false idols to take their place.

The book you hold in your hands proclaims a vision of the Law that our time has allowed to languish. In other times, when people had more refined and sophisticated ways of talking about the soul, the invisible powers that influence and shape everyday life were imagined as Gods. Humans more readily accepted themselves as mortals and recognized that human life is rarely in our control and is not subject to the heroic will that the modern mind mistakenly believes to be in charge. The stories of myth and legend remain as testaments to these earlier views, giving us precise and complex stories of the invisibles that constitute psychological life, a far cry from the dry, lifeless, and condescending theories of modern humanism and the pseudo-scientific psychologies it uses to enforce its hubris. This book harkens back to the old ways of myth and mystery, challenging the knowledge we pretend to possess. This book goes full tilt against the windmills of self-help and claims of human superiority, insisting instead that we are neither superior nor inferior to the other creatures of the earth but only one ensouled animal among many ensouled animals. That it rubs us wrong to be so compared to our fellow earthly creatures is an indicia of the mistaken pride of our age.

This book claims that the Law is one of the invisible determinants of psychological life, a psychological reality in its own right. Even this claim pales before the old language, so allow me to restate my thesis in words that speak directly to the soul. The Law belongs to the Gods, is given with the immortals, and is one of the many invisible powers that make our world possible. My claim is that the Law is a natural attribute of the soul, and so has allegiances with beautiful things, not the twisted and perverse views and conduct that have come to pass for Law. How sad that we think of our prisons as proof of our devotion to justice when they are blemishes showing the mutual degradation of the soul of the Law in our time. How obvious it is to any who will look with honest eyes that our rules and regulations are rarely intended to serve the Law's interests, but instead are designed to protect our self-interests from the competing hoards that our current ideas say surround us. That neighbors can no longer talk to one another because they fear an almost inevitable escalation to violence should tell us how far we have fallen, how weak the Law has become in our hearts.

The usual move in our time would be next to point the finger of blame. The lay public does so by claiming that lawyers and politicians are to blame. Lawyers and politicians respond that they are only the victims of bad press and poor publicity, implying in adolescent fashion that it is everyone else who is at fault. But when the issue is that our actions are insulting the Gods, then the time for finger-pointing is past. Many cultures say that without the gift of Law given by the Gods there can be no civilization. If so, it is time for hubris to be replaced by humility, and for us to redirect the energy wasted in our petty squabbles to the necessary task of restoring the crumbling walls of the Temple of Justice. Said Heraclitus, a "people should fight for their laws as for their city wall," recognizing that without Law there can be no protection from the harsher things of the world, no sense of interiority or community, no chance for enduring settlement. Compare this to the childish bickering that often passes for modern jurisprudence. How have we forgotten so much?

According to Plato, it was Zeus's gift of the moral sense that preserved humanity from self-destruction, saving us from our fear of one another. This suggests that it is not we who make the Law (the modern secular view), but that it is we who are given its blessings from powers beyond our imagination. The Law is not an abstraction, not a top-down mandate from the heights of Capitol Hill, Mount Sinai, Higher Courts, or Mount Olympus, not an oppressive regimen of restrictions and rules drawn up to benefit those who have the power to make them. The Law that this book seeks to rekindle is given with our natures, showing itself in the simple acts of kindness, good manners, and compassion that mark a civilized people. Instead of thinking of the Law as abstract, then, we would do better to imagine it as organic, bred in the bone, part of the natural world given with the soul.

In the old language, the soul was often called *mediatrix,* an in-between perspective that reflected, and thus held together, the spirit's abstract, transcending nature and the mundane, physical world of everyday bodily life. Without this middle place of soul, it was imagined, spirit and body spin off into excess, spawning, for example, fundamentalism and ideology on one hand, gluttonous materialism and heartless environmental pollution on the other. Sound familiar? Only soul enables the transcendent and the immanent to return from the exile dictated by modern dualism to commune together in a vibrant and animated (ensouled) world, precisely given, carefully crafted, sensually alive, beautiful in thought and deed.

In our lean and mean modern world, of course, the soul's work of mediation has been replaced by litigation. Where the former urges embrace and communication, enjoying the opportunities that arise from multiple viewpoints, the latter poisons life with continuing sweat and strife, all in the misguided effort to "win." Indeed the word litigation itself tries to tell us this, deriving as it does from old roots meaning "to carry on strife." But the Law given with soul avoids this heroic rhetoric of battle, instead looking for ways to overcome the "either/or" choices so often posited by competing interests that have made the age-old error of believing only in themselves.

This book encourages a renewed respect for the Law without need of such belief. The Gods have never required our belief, and have asked only to be remembered. Do we have it in us? Can we remember that in almost every classical image of Justice, her sword remains at her side instead of poised to strike a blow? Of course force is sometimes necessary for Law, and there are times when mediation is ineffective. But the Law given with our natures would not have us lash out in the first instance, convinced by my beliefs that others must be either friends or foes, with us or against us. The Law given with soul does not require such decision, no matter what our mean-spirited litigious views might proclaim to the contrary. Nor does the Law require choices between alternatives imagined by our Darwinian world-view to be necessarily in competition. And, though it is sad even to have to say it, the Law does not reside on a ledger sheet, the result of cost/benefit analyses and market forces. The Law is a gift from the Gods given to us so we might do something wonderful. It is nothing less than the aesthetic arrangement of the world, guided by images and ideas of great beauty and even greater mystery. It is a tool, like the painter's brush or a teacher's love, that holds forth the opportunity to leave a world more beautiful than before, graced by the touch of hands in service, not to ourselves and our desires, but to the Gods and their eternal aspirations.

And so this book, filled as it is with simple ideas and observations, nonetheless urges questions of ultimate concern. It urges us to consider that without Law civilization ends, and that without civilization the world will be lost to inhumane efficiencies no longer disciplined by the Gods' guiding hands. It claims that without the support of the invisibles that give face to the world we humans simply are inadequate to the many opportunities that can be ours. Soul brings talk of beauty and love, urging us toward the great things that a heart so filled can accomplish. But without beauty we will lose our ability to savor the world in its sensual fullness; without love we will grow small and mean; and without soul we are dead even though we might walk.

Only the godly powers can give us the courage, grace, and ability needed to craft a more beautiful world. Only they can teach us a love directed away from our needs to those of the world of which we are but a part. We are servants here, and when we forget this fact we become tyrants gorging on tasteless beliefs that can neither nurture nor satisfy. The Law given with soul cannot tolerate such tyranny, and this book seeks to encourage us in the eternal work of furthering the Law's noble ends.

The essays you are about to read have been written over many years and without an eye toward collection. And yet, reading them now I find that they echo certain themes and address recurring concerns. That they gather together in such a fashion is further evidence of the camaraderie of ideas. Like people, ideas have preferred associations, some ideas being of kindred spirit while others have a difficult time being together. You will find no talk here, for example, of getting it all together, becoming centered and well-related, working on relationships, boosting self-esteem, accelerating the climb for success, or figuring out personal dynamics in the name of personal gain. Such ideas are unrelated to the soul and its needs, and reflect instead our age's abiding preoccupation with the Self and its flat reflections. Instead, you will find talk of Gods and invisible powers, of the need for proper responses and appropriate conduct. It is a paltry thing, and a mistake of incalculable danger, to ignore the Gods so that we might hear our own voices more clearly. And so in many ways this is a handbook of divine service, echoing the old question to the oracle: "To which god or goddess or hero do I sacrifice." From the very beginning, it seems, we have known that discerning the powers responsible for suffering is the first step toward crafting a suitable response.

Part One addresses those most obvious servants of the Law, lawyers. Through their struggles we may all learn much of what it means to enlist our lives in the service of something beyond stock portfolios and retirement plans. If the studies and reports are accurate, lawyers are suffering inordinately in these modern times. I suspect this is because, like canaries in the mine, their increased sensitivity to the Law makes them the first to fall when the Law is starved of its needed inspiration. So I ask that you read this section not in an attempt to learn more about lawyers, but to learn more about the Law and the nature of the service it requires. Both tradition and history teaches that lawyers are far more akin to clergy and those dedicated to religious callings than they are to predatory capitalists and entrepreneurial fast-talkers. Part One explores the difficult questions of how lawyers seek to live with their calling.

Part Two expands our vision, moving from lawyers to the structures and ideas that dominate the practice of law in our time. Again, each of us has much to learn from how those devoted to serving the Law have attempted to order their service. Unfortunately, the professions and organizations that serve the Law are carried by the same muddied currents that underlie our age. And so we will see that the Law must often work to stem such currents. Only a Law true to itself can provide ideas and structures of sufficient beauty and power to counteract the cultural deformities of our time, deformities that would replace the Law's desire for communal life with personal advancement, and loyal service with bottom line fixations on profit. Part Two urges that only a courage derived from the Gods can enable us to craft a legal system worthy of the name.

Finally, in Part Three, we will turn to the world writ large. So rare is it to hear a psychologist talk of worldly matters that this section might be the most challenging to our modern perspectives. But the old view is that the world itself is ensouled, a beautiful *anima mundi* (ensouled world) full of gods and mystery. Only the paucity of modern thought has reduced the soul to the human and the human to history. We will see instead that the world is alive with soul, and that the Law is essential to its survival and well-being. Law and Order go together like one breath follows another, but we will see that the Order preferred by Law is not the order of autocratic regimentation but rather the order of the *kosmos,* an old word for order that denoted a worldly order of careful arrangement dedicated to aesthetic ends, the way a vase of flowers teaches the arranger how things might be more beautifully placed.

And so I thank you in advance, dear reader, for your interest and industry. It is not easy, this countercultural life. But ease may not be our determinant when the soul goes wanting. The life of the Law is a life of service on behalf of soul, and although the soul of the Law suffers today, let us imagine that such will not always be the case. I ask you to be a fellow advocate for the soul of the Law, standing against ideas that neglect or abuse the Law and championing those that do its bidding. I know that we live in a time where such standing is difficult, but there is no courage greater than that given by the Gods.

PART ONE

Schooled in the Habits of Worry

IT HAS BECOME the tradition of psychological inquiry to focus on the person and his or her "problems." This interest in the pathological aspects of human life, its suffering and disturbance, can offer much insight into the soul because it views the soul at its extremes. The careful precision of finding out just where it hurts and then finding ways of attending to this hurt is one of the great talents of psychology, teaching us to respect the extraordinary and the strange.

But nowadays we look through eyes clouded by the narcissism of our age, forgetting that the soul's suffering belongs first to it, and only later to us. Because we now tend to reduce all things to the human, we continuously make the error of assuming that because something feels personal it must be personal. This reduction of the psychological to the personal is one of the catastrophic mistakes of our time, leaving us nowhere to go but to an "inside," secret Self imagined as divorced from the larger world. This form of introspection leads to a devastating introversion, shrinking the cosmos into my personal skin and skull.

Another view is to turn to the suffering we experience as a way of learning more about the soul and its needs. This simple step of relieving the human from identifying with his or her symptoms opens up a range of responses unavailable to more egocentric styles of psychology. It enables us to consider that perhaps our symptoms are on to something, that they are intelligent and intelligible, sending us carefully crafted images designed to deepen our connections with the world of which we are a part.

The essays in this section begin with issues and concerns that haunt lawyers, bringing conflict into their minds and lives. But then these so-called personal issues are placed against the deeper, more basic ideas that inhabit the soul. That lawyers fall prey to habitual patterns of thought and reaction is a testament to the autonomy and power of such ideas. Our habits have us, not the other way around, so this section encourages a more honest engagement with our mental habits, recognizing their influence in our lives and in the larger ways of the world. Perhaps we suffer because our mental habits suffer, and our minds ache because the ideas that comprise them have grown cramped and weak.

The False Divide

DURING HER confirmation hearings, Attorney General Janet Reno said that although she was personally opposed to capital punishment she would continue to press for its imposition. The media, ever alert for controversy, widely reported this statement—you could tell that they were looking for a bite—but nothing, absolutely nothing happened. What is of psychological interest here is not Attorney General Reno's position, but the public acceptance of it. No one was surprised that she was able to split her views between personal, privately held beliefs and public, professional responsibilities.

Not so long ago, I spoke at a conference on hiring practices within large law firms. It was attended by hiring partners and recruitment administrators from around the country, representing a broad spectrum of large firms. A recurring topic of conversation at the conference was how a firm might put its best foot forward during the recruiting process, and in particular how to involve the more personable partners while shielding recruits from partners who "weren't so good at working with associates." During my talk I suggested that such efforts could backfire by creating unrealistic expectations, and might even erode a firm's sense of individual integrity by overemphasizing its public persona. One hiring partner responded by saying that it was easy for me to say such things because "I wasn't practicing law anymore."

What struck me most about this comment was its assumption that practicing law requires maintaining a split between a person's honest views and a public persona handcrafted to fit whatever situation is at hand. But also notable was the group's quiet acceptance of this assumption, just as with Ms. Reno's remarks.

Taken together, these two examples point to a characteristic of the legal mind. More than most people, lawyers tend to draw a sharp line between their personal and professional lives. Ethically, our codes of responsibility tell us that we are not responsible for our client's views and conduct. Professionally, we are expected to advocate a client's cause with disregard of our own beliefs (except in the most egregious of cases). If asked a question, we sometimes preface our answer by noting that we are "speaking as a lawyer," implying that we therefore are speaking in a non-personal, objective, professional manner.

This division of self is often useful. Certainly it provides an ethically defensible basis for representing clients in whom we don't believe, a task some say is necessary to the fair administration of justice. But there are troubling psychological implications in maintaining this division of self. Here are three.

First, we know that it is a false divide. There is ample proof that it isn't possible for any human to split off beliefs and attitudes into clearly defined personalities (absent psychosis, that is). The effort to nonetheless maintain the appearance of such a division creates a moral tension that every lawyer feels. It is inherent in the whole idea of legal representation that the words we say and the causes we pursue are not our own. They are the client's words translated into the language of legal representation. Intellectually we understand the jurisprudential theory underlying our actions, but emotionally we feel a conflict between our personal views and those that we are espousing publicly. (One lawyer told me that this kind of emotional conflict was "unprofessional." He said he had never felt such a conflict, and that he "never thought about it." This kind of emotional numbness and moral unconsciousness is another possible consequence of concretizing the personal/professional split.)

Second, well over half of all lawyers complain about not having enough time to spend with themselves, their families, and their friends. A common lament among young lawyers is that they are expected to "sacrifice" their personal lives to their firm. I have heard many lawyers in counseling say that their professional lives are "not enough," or that their cases lack meaning and are "just about which faceless corporation gets to keep the most money." This sense of being torn between private needs and public duty obviously has deep reverberations throughout the lawyer's life. Also, this tendency to talk about things in abstract terms ("cases," "corporations," "money") reveals a lack of visceral connection between the lawyer and his or her work. When this happens, both sides of the divide weaken. Pathology sets in. Reduced to cold, lifeless, and abstract terms, there is little wonder that work then becomes a place for incivility, misconduct, and ethical violation—after all, what difference does it make? Seen as an intimate haven to be protected, personal life loses its communal context, feels left out, peripheral. Locked within a penumbra of privacy, life becomes sanctimonious, irresponsible, vain, lonely. Psychological maturation stops as the split personalities spin their separate wheels.

Lastly, maintaining the false divide weakens professional responsiveness because its polarizing tendencies encourage division over diversity, opposition over opportunity, and competition over compromise. Worse, it cuts professional life off from its basis in the vitality of everyday life. Legal representation must include a sympathetic understanding of both the client's case and the client. Not agreement, necessarily, but understanding. But this sympathetic understanding cannot be achieved through the limited capabilities of legal analysis alone. What is required is the ability to imagine ourselves in the client's shoes, to think the client's thoughts, to feel the client's feelings. The false divide curtails sympathy and opposes the imagination that makes sympathy possible.

The distinctions we make between private and public, personal and professional, are distinctions of convenience. They are operational distinctions, made to further underlying assumptions and goals. They are not real distinctions, just as the lawyer is not really two people, lawyer and non-lawyer. Perhaps we could imagine these distinctions in more political terms, as borders joining different sovereignties. This would create new concerns. How open should the borders be? Do they cut across artificial lines, or do they denote naturally existing communities? Our responsibilities would change too, necessarily becoming both communal and individual. We would have to learn to walk the fine line between openness and protectionism. And to mark well imperialistic designs.

Minding the Store

IF YOU COULD DO or be anything in the world, what would it be? Just for a moment, forget about any limitations you might have and follow your imagination. What would your perfect-life fantasy be? The important thing about this game is to be very precise. Once you get an image of your perfect life, try to refine it. Try to imagine what an average day would be like. Try to be very particular. What time would you get up? What kind of clothes would you put on? Where would you be living? Are there other people in your life?

The first temptation is to go big—rock star, astronaut, President, shortstop. But most of these kinds of fantasies focus only on a small part of what such a life would *really* be like. Someone might love the idea of belting out a song in front of a screaming crowd, for example, but not like other parts of the rock star fantasy—the hours spent practicing, the loneliness of hopping from one dull hotel room to the next, or the frustration of living out of a suitcase for months on end.

When people start to imagine an average Wednesday in their perfect life, they sometimes find that it doesn't sound so hot after all. Sometimes, the more they think about it the more their fantasies begin to take on more down-to-earth qualities. Sometimes, their fantasies start to seem, in theory at least, actually *doable.*

But even if a person's perfect-life fantasy is objectively impossible (maybe our would-be rock star can't carry a tune), often there are qualities and aspects of the fantasy that a person can incorporate into their everyday lives in other forms.

For example, maybe part of the appeal of the rock star fantasy is being able to cut loose in front of other people, to sing from the heart. Surely such things are doable on a smaller stage.

It is easy to forget that it is the nature of our imagination that defines us, our secret dreams that sustain us. As Goethe said, "Tell me what you long for and I'll tell you who you are." Only by imagining life in the fullness of the soul's desires can our true identity begin to emerge.

Ron, for example, has been feeling increasingly listless about his legal practice. He still likes practicing law but says that he can't get over feeling that something important is missing in his life. He says he's really getting fed up with all of the paperwork and whatnot. At first, Ron said he had no idea what his perfect-life fantasy would be. I asked him to think about it, and he was quiet for a long time. Then he brightened and said he would run a hardware store in a small town.

"What would it be like to run a hardware store?"

"It would be great. I'd get up early in the morning and walk to work. I'd say hello to neighbors along the way, maybe stop and talk for a while. They'd be my customers, too. At one time or another they'd all come into the store for supplies or advice on fixing this or that."

"What about the store itself?"

"It would have everything—tools, plumbing fixtures, yard stuff, everything. It'd be an old-style store, the kind where nails are sold from big bins instead of in those little plastic things. But I'd have new stuff, too."

As it turned out, Ron had never worked in a hardware store, and for that matter didn't really know much about hardware. But his fantasy was beautifully complete.

In fact, one of the things that struck me about it was the degree to which it was complete. As Ron said, his hardware store had "everything." It even came complete with a small town in which neighbors knew each other, had time to talk, and trusted one another's counsel.

The hardware store also involved Ron in the routine things of everyday life. Walking to work, sweeping the sidewalk out front, tidying the shelves, taking inventory, ordering supplies—such chores were important. Just as it was important to help a customer to buy just the right thing to make a repair, a repair that Ron would never see. The deep satisfaction of Ron's fantasy seemed to depend on such details.

Even if Ron never learns a thing about hardware, he still can partake in the satisfactions of his hardware store fantasy by finding ways to nurture the fantasy in his everyday life. Maybe he could look at his law practice *as if* it were his hardware store. Maybe he could imagine his office desk as a countertop over which he gives advice and sells his wares. (One has to wonder, after all, why Ron values giving advice about leaky faucets more than he values the advice he gives to his real-life clients.) He could pay more attention to daily maintenance and the nuts and bolts of everyday legal practice, especially because these are the very areas of his professional life in which he has lost interest. Surely monotony has a place in running the store.

Maybe the next time Ron answers a client's simple question without charge he could see it as a neighborly act, all the time remaining secure in the knowledge that the neighbor would be back in later for nails and paint. He could see doing monthly billings as going over the accounts. He might even start paying more attention to the actual hardware of his office—paper, computers, pens and pencils, whatever. Ron has a store to run, after all, and in a store you do what needs doing.

You get the idea. By following the lead of his imagination, *by allowing imagination,* Ron might find ways of living his desires in everyday life. By reconnecting his imagination with his work, both are deepened and made more meaningful, more alive. For Ron, at least, the key to a perfect life seems to be an educated imagination that can learn how to mind the store.

Things We Think We Know

I'M BIG ON thinking about what's *going* to happen. I think about the future often, doing calculations and probabilities in my head, making lists, budgets, five-year plans, writing schedules.

None of these plans ever pan out, of course. Occasionally, I'll come across an old budget that I made and be reminded of just how widely my anticipations miss the mark. The other day, I found a writing schedule that said I should almost be finished writing a book that I haven't even thought about for over a year. So it goes.

From the vantage point of the present, it is easy to see how life rarely matches the courses we chart. Life seems always to wander and veer, perhaps suggesting an overall direction, but without any clear indication of a destination. At the same time, though, these wanderings also seem to be connected in some way, to fit together, to make sense. They almost seemed destined the way biographies often seem to hold together like stories.

A man came to see me about a decision he had to make. Early in our conversation he said he needed to make the decision right away. I pointed out that by rushing his decision he was most likely overlooking obvious things, things that would later loom large, like a typo in a headline. In fact, the things he was missing probably would show up in the very places he now was examining most closely. Certainly, this wasn't a revelation. He knew as well as I that things seldom work out the way we have them planned, just as he knew that when we get caught up in an idea, or a decision, or a quest of some sort we can become blind to our own wisdom. But by reminding himself of these simple truths, and accepting the inevitability of his disappointments, he was able to approach his decision just a little more calmly.

The puzzle in all of this is the divergence of two supposedly closely related phenomena. On the one hand we have our best-laid plans. On the other hand we have the testament of history. They are not the same. Sometimes they might show an affinity for one another, but on the whole they often seem like two different stories.

Despite this fact, we persist in believing that planning is a literal activity. That is, we think that what we plan will *actually* happen. More, we think that because we plan something, it *must* happen, thereby interjecting into our plans a subtle moralism. Taking plans literally in this fashion creates expectations that cannot be fulfilled and gives rise to an abiding anxiety.

Another way of looking at our plans is as essentially imaginative constructions, as *works of fiction.* (Some plans, of course, like my physical fitness programs and my diets, are more fictitious than others.) From this more literary perspective, we begin to see that our plans have deeper significance for the life of the soul. Taken literally, plans can be drudging attempts at control, while those same plans, thoroughly imagined, can be statements of ambition and desire. Our plans teach us much about our ideals, about how we think about the world, and about what matters most to us. Ask yourself, What is the nature of my planning? When I think about the future, in what terms do I tend to think? Do I focus on things like money, fitness, and success? Or do my thoughts go to family and friends? What ideals, ambitions, and desires are hidden in my plans? What am I truly hoping for?

The great thing about planning is that you can really let your imagination go because there's no way in hell that things are going to happen the way you plan them. Like the man with the rushed decision, once we acknowledge the inevitability of changing circumstances we can become more relaxed, maybe even playful, about our planning. Instead of being rigid standards of measurement that cause anxiety about meeting abstract expectations, plans can provide ways for us to celebrate our fictional talents, ways of imagining the future and our place in it. Our plans, and history's comic treatment of them, can instill in us a reflective awareness that our personal desires have little impact on the actual outcome of our lives. They can remind us that things are never only as they seem, and that there are other, invisible forces at work that ultimately determine our destiny. Tradition teaches that there is a thread for each of us in Fate's tapestry, a thread whose length is unknown even to the Gods.

Our plans also show us how things of no apparent consequence can later blossom in ways we never could have guessed. It strikes me as one of life's marvels that the smallest act can carry untold consequences. We cannot know what is important, not now, not ever. Even the lives of those long dead are sources for constant reinterpretation as our imaginings about history are rewoven over time.

Often in therapy, someone will remind me of something I said in a previous session. It almost always is something that I didn't think was important at the time, something that I never would have remembered. In fact, if you had asked me what that earlier session was about, I probably would have focused on some big idea or image that I was trying to get across. But the soul tends to ignore such grandiose efforts and instead hears significance in little things, little asides.

Our plans, and especially our failed plans, are evidence of

the essential role that imagination plays in the life of the soul. They teach us that we rarely, if ever, know for sure what we are doing, or what small action is going to matter to the soul. Plans offer a possibility for imagining the unseen destiny at work in our daily lives, and remind us that the brighter our projections the more blind we become to what is happening in the dark.

Fateful Feelings

THE OTHER DAY, a friend of mine was telling me about a visit he had with his therapist. My friend had confided to the therapist a secret belief he harbored about himself, a belief, and please note the words here, that he felt "destined" to do something big, something important. The problem was that my friend had no idea what that something was. Nonetheless, he believed deep inside that he was meant to do something . . . significant.

After listening to this confession, my friend's therapist said, somewhat offhandedly according to my friend, that "everybody felt like that," and then proceeded to change the subject to something more to the therapist's liking, namely my friend's childhood. My friend was a little offended by the therapist's dismissal, and even felt a bit humiliated, as if he had revealed an arrogance. The therapist seemed to be implying that my friend's sense that his life was somehow fated was either narcissistic and grandiose or too common a feeling to be worthy of psychological interest.

I beg to differ. It seems to me that my friend wasn't necessarily being grandiose. It's my hunch that deep down inside we all feel that we are unique, destined, fated, meant for something we know not what. I think we all know, in our heart of hearts, that no one else has ever experienced the world in quite the same way and that we have things to offer that no one else does.

My friend's therapist was right that the feeling of destiny is a common experience. But he was wrong to dismiss it on this basis. We have to remember that it is on the surface of our most common experiences that we find traces of the soul's deepest currents. Surely every life, no matter how unreported or obscure, feels the demands of Fate. Surely every life feels imprinted with divine intentions, making it always partly immortal, partly mythical. Surely every life actualizes the eternal.

Such ideas are hard for us. At first blush they sound too esoteric, maybe even religious, to be trusted. The idea of destiny grits our teeth because it conflicts with our overriding beliefs in the absoluteness of the individual and his or her inalienable rights. Destiny, to this way of thinking, threatens freedom itself by calling into question the autonomy of the individual will. Just look at the old and continuing debate between proponents of predestination and free-will, an egocentric diversion if ever there was one.

The very bigness of the idea of destiny also alarms us. God knows we have seen enough crazies who have done great harm while following some deranged fantasy of their own self-importance. There have been too many Hitlers, too many Mansons, too many Big Shots wielding destiny as a sword for us not to be wary.

But to *assume,* as my friend's therapist did, that all feelings of destiny are really egotism in disguise is to deny intractable feelings. It is a modern conceit, after all, that it is we who create the Gods. Throughout human time, people everywhere have felt the pull and push of destiny. Quite apart from this or that philosophical stance, the *experience* of destiny remains a simple fact of life.

Let's step away from the quagmires before we get sucked into yet another argument over the sovereignty of the individual. Mine is a simpler point. When I look back over my life, I am struck, like my friend, that it seems to cohere in certain discernible ways. No matter how wild things might have seemed at the time, or how unpredictable the future remains, in retrospect the events of my life seem to fit together. I don't mean that they remain static, of course, because we all know that over time the same events take on different meanings. Rejection becomes defensiveness becomes humility becomes a source of strength, and so on. And yet in the midst of my life's ever-changing mosaic there is a sense of sameness, as if looking through a particular kaleidoscope.

Individuality emerges from such retrospection like a dominant color, a particular rhythm, or a distinctive combination of spices. This is the kind of individuality I think we point to when we say an author or other artist has "found their voice," a kind of individuality woven of the unique and the familiar. If each of us could tell our life's story, I am convinced we would be astounded both by how intricate and precious they are, and by how much they remind us of one another.

To the degree that in each life we discern the work of unseen hands, we come to see the aesthetic potential in everyday experience. Something is being made. Life as opus. Imagine how life might be if we saw every little act as a dropped pebble sending ripples to foreign shores. Imagine if we viewed the work of our lives as making biography.

I mean none of this in the grandiose way feared by my friend's therapist. Destiny brings with it a powerful and paradoxical responsibility. We are both blameless and liable. On the one hand, because we can't know the significance of our actions while they are happening, we have no choice but to act as we will. On the other hand, because every act holds historic potential, it behooves us to be more considerate of what we do. We never know what foundations are being laid or what story lines set into motion.

The physicists tell us that every action has a reaction. If so, which are we? Caught up in the routine bustle of everyday life, it is easy to forget that the things we do now are the things by which we will be remembered later, the things that will become our legacy. Perhaps that is one of the things our fateful feelings are trying to tell us, that destiny lies in the remembering.

Pulling the Thread

THERE IS A RECURRING theme in the legal imagination that is best presented through its clichés: don't open the door, don't ask one question too many, don't ask a question you don't know the answer to, don't open that can of worms, don't start down that slippery slope, don't open those floodgates, and don't pull that thread. And don't forget that you can't unring a bell.

All of these catch-phrases remind the lawyer to be careful, and emphasize how important, and difficult, it is to stick to the point. Few things in lawyering are as critical as being able to present your case without distraction or deviation.

Just think how much of the sparring that takes place during a trial is about timing, about throwing the opponent off stride. The goal is to make our story compelling and sensible while making our opponent's story appear disjointed and incredible. The skilled adversary therefore is trained to reiterate and reinforce his or her position, and, as the salespeople put it, to Always Be Closing.

There is something beautiful about the precise and deliberate actions of good trial lawyers. They seem so sure-footed, and to know just how far to go. There is something almost instinctual about how they avoid temptations and stay doggedly on track. This ability to concentrate on telling one's story in a decided way while also watching for potential diversions is one of the great talents of the legal imagination.

The restraint involved in all of this also is admirable. The legal mind is characterized by curiosity if nothing else, and it takes quite an effort for a lawyer to refrain from exploring every avenue of inquiry. The main reason lawyers have trouble not asking the next question is that they delight so in asking questions.

But there is more going on here. The effort it takes to tell a story at trial also is a reflection of the artificiality of the process. No story can really be confined to the courtroom, nor for that matter to the issues the lawyers want to argue about. No true story has hemmed edges; they are naturally frayed, naturally prone to unraveling. And no one knows this better than the lawyer. Every lawyer knows how intricate and multilayered life is, how full of potential and pressure. Every lawyer knows that sometimes all it takes is a pin-prick.

I've heard police officers say that the degree to which two or more witnesses tell the same story is a good indication of their collaboration and deceit. It simply isn't natural for two people to witness the same event and then tell exactly the same story. There always is something different in their tellings.

Part of the effort that goes into a trial, then, lies in sustaining an unusual focus. We ask juries to pay attention to things in a way they aren't used to. We ask them to confine themselves to this set of facts, to pay attention to this, not that, and to believe us in what we say is important. The great challenge facing the lawyer is to tell a coherent story that comports with the jury's experience while also supporting the lawyer's position. And yet, at the same time, good trial lawyers know that the story cannot be too pat or too tightly woven or it will seem artificial. If it isn't just a little messy, it will not be believed. Part of the lawyer's artistry lies in trying to control where this mess appears, and to intentionally provide places where the jury's mind *can* wander, places that are safe for the lawyer's position. If such places can also be turned to advantage by providing room for the jury to come up with their own damaging theories about the opponent's case, so much the better. Nothing is quite as devastating to a lawyer's carefully crafted case as a jury that goes off on its own, because it is almost impossible to rebut an implication.

I wonder, though, about the psychological implications of this professional mindset in lawyers' non-legal lives. After all, there is undoubtedly a kind of paranoia about all of this. We don't open the door because we are afraid of what is or might be behind it; we don't ask one question too many because we are afraid of the answer we might get; we don't pull the thread because we are afraid everything will come undone, and so on. Such caution might make all the sense in the world in an adversarial context, but elsewhere it can cause problems.

Many lawyers report feeling inadequate and inferior in interpersonal relationships. Many non-lawyers describe lawyers as guarded and aloof and say that lawyers are reluctant to be intimate.

I suspect that the deep-seated reticence people sense in lawyers actually is part and parcel of the legal imagination. When we see a funny look on our partner's face but stop ourselves from asking what's up, are we not unconsciously following our legal training by refusing to open the door? Surely what sounds to us like not asking one question too many sounds to others like disinterest. It sounds like we don't want to hear the rest of it, how it all played out. By not asking questions we don't already know the answers to we can come off looking like know-it-alls who don't care what other people think. It's like asking someone to tell you a joke and then walking away before they can give you the punch line.

It leaves the teller thwarted, frustrated, and insulted—hardly a basis for intimacy.

Sometimes it also is easy to move from not opening doors to closing them. That's the paranoia taking hold. That's when we start to see loose threads on the emperor's new clothes. But we probably shouldn't get into that. I fear I've already said too much.

Two Stories

I KNOW A LAWYER who was representing the estate of a dead doctor in a malpractice case. The players included the executor of the estate, a few ex-patients of the dead doctor, a few more insurance companies, and everybody's lawyers. The lawyer said that although everyone else seemed interested in reaching a quick settlement, she was being inexplicably hesitant in making a decision about what to do. She said she just had a "gut feeling that something was missing."

As we talked about it, I asked whether the some*thing* missing might be a some*one*. Where was the dead doctor in all of this? Was he being neglected, left out? I suggested that the lawyer imagine having a dialogue with the doctor. She could ask the doctor what he thought about the settlement. After all, the outcome of the case was going to influence the doctor's imaginal legacy. Apart from preserving the estate in quantitative terms, wasn't the lawyer also charged with preserving the doctor's lasting impression? Why not ask the doctor how he wanted to be remembered?

It sounded worth a try, and the lawyer began to imagine conversations between her and the dead doctor. Their conversations are privileged, of course, but they did seem to fortify the lawyer's resolve. She told me that she occasionally imagined the doctor being present at certain times. She even joked that she wanted to set a place at the table for the doctor at the next negotiation, and then pause from time to time to confer with him. We wondered what the other people at the table would hear in those moments of silence.

Another lawyer told me about a case he was working on in which his client was extremely emotionally involved. It seemed the more the lawyer told the client not to worry the more anxious the client became. Finally, without really thinking about it, the lawyer gave his home phone number to the client. The lawyer said that the effect of this simple act on the client was immediately apparent. Although the client remained concerned about the case, sometimes to the point of anxiety, the relationship between the two men had changed. *The client trusted the lawyer.* It was as if the lawyer had suddenly been revealed to the client's mind as a real person, a person who cared about the client's plight and who was trying to help. By offering private access, the lawyer had somehow bridged the gap that so often separates lawyer from client.

Given this experience, the lawyer started giving out his home phone number to other clients. As you would expect, it was usually accepted without any fanfare whatsoever. But on a few occasions it sparked a feeling of intimacy like the lawyer had felt with the first client.

These experiences also revealed to the lawyer that he was harboring some hidden feelings toward his clients. He realized how easily he became bothered and irritated when talking with clients. He realized that he had started thinking of his clients almost as abstractions, as just files and cases, or, worse, as economic opportunities. Clearly he was too distant from his clients, too out of touch.

Giving out his home phone number allowed the lawyer to feel differently about his clients. He said he felt more concerned about them than he had before. At the same time, he started feeling differently about himself. He said he felt more "like a lawyer." Opening more intimate lines of communication with his clients had infused his practice with a kind of neighborliness in which there was a greater sense of mutual concern and responsibility. All of this, and the lawyer said he could count on one hand the number of times a client has actually *used* his home phone number.

Obviously I am not suggesting that lawyers should talk to dead clients, or freely give out home phone numbers, although neither seems like such a bad idea to me. No, my point is that these simple stories demonstrate how activating imagination can encourage a deeper respect for the invisible aspects of work. And it is these invisible aspects that are work's essence, the source of its satisfaction.

One common theme in these two stories is that imagination was inspired and an aesthetic contribution to the life of the soul was made. Through work-based revelations, people became more attached to their work in unexpected ways and more aware of the mysterious undercurrents that imperceptibly flowed through their lives. They found in the midst of common experience the swell of eternal happenings, the whisper of ancestral voices, and the pleasures of simple service. To some extent, they were taken out of themselves and made aware that they were part of something else, like necessary characters in an endless work-in-progress.

Compare such feelings to how we usually look at things. The estate lawyer could have just gone along with the deal, rationalizing her decision, closing the case, and collecting her fee. Or the other lawyer could have kept his home phone number private, or given it out only because he thought it was a good "marketing" or "networking" technique. But such responses are too meager, too small to nourish the soul. They reduce our ability to *enjoy* our work by obscuring the epiphanies present there.

We must remember that work is a natural activity of the

soul, and so introduces us into destiny. Our work forever includes us in a lineage of practitioners and is one of the fundamental ways in which we contribute to the communal sweep of history. But history lies with the devil in the details. To do right by our work, right by our destinies, we must begin with the stories within the story that swirl like eddies in the backwaters of the soul. We must begin with little things, like hearing a voice in the wind, or giving ourselves freely to another.

Your Reputation Precedes You

JUST AS A PERSON cannot see his or her own face, so too we can never directly perceive our own reputations. We might catch a glimpse of our reputations, yes, but we can never get a full-faced look at them.

Part of the problem is that our interest in looking at our own reputation is usually too vain, so that what we see is always in two dimensions, like a mirror. A person's perception of his or her own reputation lacks necessary perspective and a depth of field that is available only to other people. In short, we might *think* we know what our reputation is, but we don't, we can't. Not for sure.

But wait, you say. Surely I can ask people with whom I am intimate to tell me what other people say about me. And then there are the times when I've overheard people talking about me when they didn't know I was around. And what about when other people let slip their private thoughts about me, like when I'm having a fight with someone and they say something like, "You are so stubborn! You're just like your father!" Doesn't this give me information about what my reputation is? And for that matter, Mister Psychotherapist, what about therapy itself? Isn't that one of the things I pay my therapist for, to give me an objective view of myself?

Well, I hate to disappoint all of the self-help, look-into-my-eyes-and-tell-me-the-truth folks, but I doubt seriously whether what we learn from such encounters has anything much to do with our actual reputations, much less some kind of "objective" description of who we are. The fact is that we are always like fish reflecting about life beyond our fish bowl.

The word "reputation" itself comes from roots meaning "to think about again, to reconsider." In other words, our reputations are actually reflections on us and of us in the imaginations of other people. Our reputations cannot accurately be said to be "ours" but rather are *theirs,* belonging to other people who keep and make our reputations within the confines of their own fantasies about us.

Think about the things we say: "I have my reputation to uphold," or "I have a right to protect my reputation," or "Your reputation precedes you," and so on. In each case we have evidence of the otherness of our reputations. After all, if our reputations precede us then they are only there when we are not. Catch-22.

Take two examples. In the first, you and I are close friends. We're sitting having a beer and you ask me to tell you, truthfully now, what people think about you. I demur for a while, but then, maybe after another beer, I say: "People say that you're a hot-head."

In the second example, you and I are talking about someone else. Neither of us knows the other person directly, but we know what we've heard. I say to you about the other person, "I hear he's a hot-head."

In the first case maybe you get mad or defensive (maybe they're right about you after all). In the second case we have engaged in an act of pure imagination based on nothing but the fiction of the other person's reputation. Nevertheless, this fiction will affect how we act, at least initially, if we ever meet the reputed hot-head. Who knows, maybe our initial standoffishness will make the person feel uncertain and insecure to the point that they will become defensive and actually act like a hot-head.

A person's reputation is like a fantasy twin. It may or may not have any basis in so-called fact, and it lives a life of its own out in the world, beyond the person, preceding the person. (Does this mean that our reputations know where we are going before we do?) Our reputations are our representatives in the communal imagination, and influence other people's perceptions of us. No one knows "the truth" about us, if by truth we mean some kind of historically based, objectively provable fact. Rather let us say that our reputations remind us that we are by and large figments in the world's imagination, fantasy creatures of mixed fact, myth, and story.

This last point is important—reputations are told as stories, and work at the deeper levels of metaphorical reality. Some people say that in the end our reputations are all that we have left, that it is our reputations that continue to live after we are gone, that it is our reputations that haunt the future. Maybe that is why we feel so frustrated in trying to protect our reputations; we know how much we depend on them now for our identity, and how much we will depend on them in the future for our lasting existence in memory. No wonder we can never quite set the record straight to suit us.

One reason often given for incivility among lawyers in larger urban areas is the unlikelihood that any given lawyer will have to work with any other given lawyer again in the future. I wonder if this means that we need our reputations to protect us against our own egotism? If so, then we might want to change the ways in which we think about our reputations. Instead of "building a good reputation" as a work of the ego—"look at me, look how good I am"—we might see reputation as a way of tempering the ego's natural excesses—"I think I'm a really nice guy, but word has it that I'm hard to get along with." This doesn't mean that we spend our lives chasing our reputations (although maybe that's what destiny feels like seen from behind), but it does mean that we might think a little more about the mythical dimensions of our lives and about the stories in which we take part.

On Intimacy

THE MOST COMMON psychological complaint among lawyers nationwide is a feeling of inadequacy and inferiority in interpersonal relationships. For all we know, this might be the most common psychological complaint among folks in general, but it is especially interesting that lawyers, among the most highly trained communicators in our society, should have such feelings. What is going on? Why do lawyers have so much trouble entering and sustaining intimate relationships?

We take a lead from the poet Rainer Marie Rilke:

> I hold this to be the highest task of a bond between two people: that each should stand guard over the solitude of the other.

Elsewhere, Rilke returned to this idea:

> All companionship can consist only in the strengthening of two neighboring solitudes, whereas everything that one is wont to call giving oneself is by nature harmful to relationship. . . .

What extraordinary ideas! That the task of relationship is *not* the fulfillment of our personal desires, but the fulfilling of another person's desires. Put otherwise, the secret to intimacy, according to Rilke, lies not in being intimate *ourselves,* but in creating a place where another person can be intimate.

Now this might sound obvious, but think how it goes against the grain of what usually passes for advice and counseling on relationships. We are told to be open about our needs, to share our feelings, to tell the other person what we want, and so on . . . all of that hand-holding and eye-gazing. And yet here is Rilke telling us that these attitudes and approaches are too self-centered and self-interested; they imply that relationships are there for *us*, when in fact the idea is to devote ourselves to the soul of another, to stand guard over that soul in its moments of solitude and weakness, not hovering, not doting, but attending, watching—and then standing back when the other person's soul moves, appreciating it for the rare bird that it is. Nice ideas. Imagine relationships freed from our self-absorption, free from the demands of sharing, free from having to be fulfilling, free from being some kind of mushy union between two people not considered good enough in their own right, free to be adult, free to take flight. Here relationship becomes another thing, a third thing that exists between people, and it becomes our job to serve the relationship, not vice versa.

All of this implies that intimacy is not a job of the ego alone. The ego tends to fall into itself too much, and so needs help from other quarters in matters of the heart. Relationships are notoriously irrepressible, taking their own course beyond the frustrated ego's control. And they tend to speak a language that is difficult for the ego. Intimate relationships, as the words themselves tell us, proceed through intimation. To "intimate" something is to proceed indirectly, not to say it straight out, and so we do a disservice to relationships when we ask them to be fully explicated, and demand that the people within them be completely open and honest. This view betrays a paranoia, a deep suspicion that believes relationships are safe only when they are expressions of mutual surrender, on our backs, baring our throats. But hear Rilke:

> When a person abandons himself, he is no longer anything, and when two people both give themselves up in

> order to come close to each other, there is no longer any ground beneath them and their being together is a continual falling.

Surely Rilke is correct. Surely it takes strength to stand guard over the solitude of another and to give up our insistent demands for personal satisfaction. Surely there is love worth dying for.

So what about us lawyers then? Well, it doesn't take much reflection to realize that we are educated and trained to view relationships in terms of what might go wrong. One of the great services that lawyers offer their clients is precisely this prophylactic approach—to go slow, consider the angles, and watch for pitfalls. What if the other side is lying? What if they're hiding something? What if they aren't telling the whole story? And so on.

We also are educated and trained to prefer, indeed to demand, clear and straightforward language. Not that we don't twist and turn every word, of course, but the *fantasy* is that we are being rational and clear. We don't trust metaphors or poetic phrases because they are too ambiguous, too open to too many meanings. Again, all of this makes sense within the rarefied air of legal practice, where the still prevalent attitude toward relationships is that they are places ripe with conflict and adversity.

The problem comes when we allow these professional attitudes to seep into the groundwater of our everyday lives. Thinking about a relationship in terms of what can go wrong might make sense in a legal transaction but clearly is inappropriate in matters intimate. Demanding the truth, the whole truth, and nothing but the truth might make sense from a witness, but it is boorish when applied to the simple graces of daily love.

There are other similar problems, of course. In legal practice, for example, we are expected to be closed, careful, and circumspect. From this perspective, intimate relationships are naturally going to be seen as too open-ended, wild, and exposing. We also have to be aware of the lawyer's tendency to apply a legalistic overlay to things in general, an overlay that is truly appropriate only in certain particular situations (which generally do not include hushed, candle-lit moments).

But "to stand guard over the solitude of the other." That's the ticket. You see how this simple admonition frees us from all of our self-centered concerns. It no longer is a matter of me. Intimacy shifts us to concerns about the other, about their soul's desires. We become devotees, caretakers of a different sort, serving the relationship as a temple of soul-making.

How Does Your Garden Grow?

I TALK WITH lots of people who, if not unhappy in what they do, are hardly thrilled to get up in the morning and go to work. Most of these people would likely be considered middle or upper-middle class, and appear from the outside to live comfortable and stable lives. When you talk to them about their work, they assume a more or less workmanlike attitude toward things. Sure, they have to take some crap at work, but the pay is good, and they are pretty good at what they do, too. Sometimes the social status associated with their work is a further inducement for them to continue what they're doing.

So far, no problem. It's their life, right? But sometimes, every now and then, it won't be all right. Maybe late at night, as they lie awake staring at the ceiling, or after a birthday or anniversary, or when bad news arrives out of the blue, these people can suddenly become disillusioned. "What am I doing?" they ask incredulously. "How did I get here?" I don't mean that they ask these questions in a depressed or confused way, either. There often is a certain clarity of thought surrounding such moments. These are basic questions, questions having religious significance, and the clarity of thought and perception that accompanies them can have the feeling of a revelation.

The answer to these heartfelt questions usually is "I don't know." Oh, we might tell stories about being pressured into our career by our parents, or point to a long history of education and training that makes our current state seem a logical conclusion, but at base we don't really feel like we were *meant* to be doing what we are doing.

Many lawyers have told me they "fell into" practicing law. Law offered an outlet for their intelligence and energy, the potential for a nice income, and ready-made social standing. But they weren't really in love with the law or anything like that. It was just a nice alternative.

Such people rarely feel that what they are doing is in accord with their destiny. In fact, they probably don't have much of a sense of destiny at all, and might even make fun of such notions. But it is precisely this lack of awe and wonder about their lives that leaves their personal history feeling like mere happenstance.

One fall, my wife bought some bulbs to plant in our garden for the following spring and summer. She had written on little slips of paper the exact types of the various plants, along with the color of their blooms, and all of this was organized neatly beside our back porch—until we had some yard work done, that is, and the workmen kindly rearranged things for us, putting the slips of paper in a neat stack beside a jumbled pile of bulbs. The upshot was that the bulbs had to be planted with little or no idea of what was going to come up.

This is an apt analogy for what many people go through in many parts of their lives. Seeds are planted, tended, and nurtured perhaps for years, and then, when the seeds finally mature, we realize they weren't the plants we wanted to start with. I mean, why did I grow broccoli? I hate broccoli! And now all I've got is broccoli!

The question is what to do about it. Here you are in a field of broccoli that represents the investment of years of your life. It's probably a very nice garden. In fact, it might be heaven for someone who likes broccoli. But it just isn't your taste.

In a real garden, it might be frustrating to dig something up and move it elsewhere, but it usually isn't that big a deal. But when a person realizes they have grown a life other than the one they really want, and looks back at the time and energy it has taken to grow that life, the thought of starting over again from seed can be daunting, if not seemingly impossible. There are so many reasons to continue growing what we've already started.

We all know how difficult it can be to walk away from the familiar, just as it can be hard to admit to ourselves that we don't like broccoli. But must we really finish everything we start? Aren't some things best left to others?

We should be careful about this "starting over" talk, though. It implies too much, as if life is supposed to be an undeflected arrow, straight and to the point. Starting over is part of the developmental fantasy that contributes to our anxiety in the first place. But there is no starting over in life, there is only life.

Another way to look at all of this is to imagine that the plants we have grown are necessary predicates to what we can grow now. It is our cultural mania, after all, that sees any change in direction as a criticism of our prior course. But what if the plants we have grown are themselves seeds of a different sort? What if there has been something within us all along that has been moving toward maturity, and this movement requires all of the false starts, detours, and breakdowns along the way? Perhaps our mistakes provide essential nutrients.

Don't get me wrong. There is nothing wrong with growing the same thing all the time if that is what the soul truly desires, just as there is nothing inherently good or preferable about change. But true morality lies in the respect one shows destiny.

Imagine your life ten years from now if you could live

exactly the life you think you would like to live. Be serious about it for a moment; no silly extravagances. Imagine the life you desire.

What seeds must be planted to grow that life? Are they seeds compatible with the field you are now working? Maybe the grass really *is* greener elsewhere. What do you want, broccoli or roses?

Three Cases

CASE ONE: Dynamic woman partner in large urban law firm, mid-forties. Said to have a real future. Comes to therapy to work out problems with parents and various relationships. Complains constantly about slights suffered in these relationships.

Case Two: Young man, age 36. Affable, easygoing in speech and mannerism, but with a certain aloofness. Is not "satisfied" with his marriage. Turns all conversation in therapy to this issue.

Case Three: Single man, age 27. General anxiety. Conscious concerns focus especially on money and self-advancement. Feels "stretched to the limit" both financially and emotionally. Has thought about suicide.

All cases are unique, and all sound general themes. In every circumstance, at least one underlying theme holds: each person is suffering from a problem with relationship. The problem with most modern psychotherapy, however, is that it misplaces, perhaps displaces, the source and nature of this relationship.

Case One would likely fall prey to reductive notions about troubled self-esteem. Case Two might be said to have a mother problem. Case Three surely is narcissistic. We could come up with a dozen or more alternative diagnoses, but still we would miss the mythical, repeating aspect of what is being said.

I have my own ideas. I believe that in Case One the woman was in the process of coming to terms with the power structures inherent in adult life. She obviously was highly skilled and savvy in the intricate, though settled, ways of the law. Her problem was in sensing these power dynamics in settings outside the firm. A concurrent complaint was a sense of not being at home when she was at home. Her mind stayed at the office. Plates went unwashed. Too many dinners came out of a box. I still wonder whether such things were not essential indications of her emotional disconnection with the world. Her problem was relational, yes, but was it limited to human relationships? My sense was she was hungry for a world to be alive in.

Enter Case Two. After too many hours of listening to this man complain about his wife, I asked him to name one thing he loved. His wife, he said. I pointed out that his wife was not a thing and that I meant an actual thing, an object. I wanted to know one object he loved. He couldn't name one single item. It broke my heart. Surely one reason this man felt such pressure in his marriage was that he expected it to contain and give form to *all* of his erotic connections with the world. Having repressed these passions, he could not love the simplest thing; how could his wife possibly carry the burden of his ungiven love? But please note, *it made more sense to him to blame his suffering on his marriage than to think he was neglecting his world.*

Which brings us to Case Three. Early in our therapy, he noted he had a garage full of items he had bought over the years. Most had to do either with the outdoors or getting ready for the outdoors: skis, a ski machine, kayaks, a rowing machine, golf clubs, etc. After a few sessions, and in an offhand manner, he said there simply "wasn't enough time to take care of things." He of course meant there were too many things going on for him to attend to. But I wondered whether this comment might also be emanating from that garage. What if the disquiet he felt was also partly a reflection of those things in the garage that, in fact, were not being taken care of. Imagine how that set of golf clubs might feel. When he bought them he was giddy with pleasure; he thought maybe they had the magic necessary to break that elusive score. And now look at them, covered over with crap and rusting to boot. Does not some part of him feel their abandonment? Perhaps, again, we have a problem of a person out of love with his world.

The significant lesson to be drawn from such cases is that what we posit as interpersonal problems often have an environmental aspect. We humans are sensitive creatures, and it should come as no surprise that we mirror the disaffections and sufferings of our world. We are part of it, after all. This means that what we feel as personal can also be seen as reflecting worldly displeasure.

In all three cases, the people involved had love problems. Their biggest problem, though, was in reducing their erotic problems to only their interpersonal relationships when it was more a problem of their relationship with the world and its things. Case One did not trust herself to exercise her worldly powers appropriately. Case Two couldn't love a compass his grandfather had given him; how could he possibly muster the love required for marriage? Case Three was living life above the earth. Despite his accumulation of worldly possessions, he was groundless and without any reference points—the very definition of anxiety.

The point is that psychology too often draws our attention away from the actual sources of our discomforts by positing the source of all psychological disturbances as within the person. This is a fundamental error. We feel washed out and assume the problem is within us, never thinking about the white walls and sunless light we sit in all day. We seem incapable of imagining that the world might be telling us something. And yet the squirrel knows just how far to jump; the bird where it hid that seed; and the cat where is the best place for a nap.

The ancients believed the human was a microcosm of the greater universe, and that what happened "out there" resonated "in here," and vice versa. In our time we have reversed this relationship, believing instead that we "project" consciousness onto a dead world, a world incapable of having a soul. That is what the people I have told you about firmly believed. What do you think?

What Are You Worth?

I'VE HAD A MEMORY in mind the past couple of days of an event that happened almost ten years ago while I was still practicing law. I was in one of the ubiquitous coffee rooms found in most law firms with one of the firm's up-and-coming partners. We had stopped off on the way to his office to get a cup of coffee. He poured me a cup, topped off his cup, and put the now-empty coffee pot back on the hot plate. Over to my left sat a middle-aged woman who appeared to be taking a break. I paused, waiting for the partner to make another pot of coffee, but he started to walk out.

Now for many years I was a waiter, and if there is one thing every waitperson hates it is somebody who won't make another pot of coffee after emptying a pot. You will find no public disagreement on this point. Such a person is a jerk, end of story. I mean, who the hell do they think they are?

"How about we make another pot?" I asked, trying to be casual. The partner looked straight at me, and said an amazing thing. It was the answer to my question about who the hell they think they are.

"I bill out at two hundred dollars an hour. It isn't worth my time to make a pot of coffee."

Well, you could have scraped me off the floor with a spatula. I simply could not believe it. My spirits rose for a moment when I thought maybe he was kidding, but no, he was not kidding, he was leaving. I slid out after him, feeling two eyes burning into my back as we left.

I never said anything more to the guy about it, but it really got to me. In fact, the more I dealt with him, the more fitting the event became (he was an exceptionally well-rounded jerk), but I never forgot it. Even now, after all of the these years, I still get hot when I think about it. Perhaps Freud was right that the repressed goes through no alteration over time.

Some things have changed, I suppose. I used to think the guy was just unbelievably pretentious and arrogant. I remember once thinking about timing myself to see how long it took to make a pot of coffee and then calculating out how much I would have had to pay him. But that seemed like an awful lot of work for a minor obsession. Now, given the money lust that tyrannizes our society, I wonder if his actions weren't even more sinister than I originally thought.

There was an article in the paper recently about a factory owner whose company had been in the family for several generations. The factory burned down, and the general fear in the town where the factory was located was that the owner would follow the modern trend and rebuild the factory overseas where troubling things like the minimum wage and safety regulations wouldn't get in the way of maximizing profit. But then the owner announced he wouldn't dream of such a thing. It turned out he was proud of his company's legacy in the town, and not only did he promise to rebuild on the old foundation, but he assured his workers they would continue to get paid in the interim. A nice story, and one that in another time might have been less conspicuous. Here was a business man who remembered that the function of a business is not only to make money.

A few days later came a letter to the editor from a disgruntled man who said if he found out a company he had invested in was doing anything with its money other than trying to maximize the value of his stock he would immediately pull his money out and put it elsewhere. He used the word "altruism" as a pejorative, equating it with "foolish," and warned that nonproductive actions such as those taken by the factory owner were a prelude to bankruptcy.

That's when I remembered the coffee pot incident. Here were two men of like mind. Money was their only standard of "worth." Screw the employees, laugh at ideas of community and loyalty. Just get me mine. Let someone else make the coffee, because on the great ledger book of life they are worth less than me. Politeness? Fairness? Decency? Please.

The most frightening aspect is that some people actually believe one's "worth" can be equated with money. Let me put it this way. Would you want that $200 an hour lawyer as a friend, a husband, a father? If he were your son, would you be proud to hear what he said to me? And what about the damage he did to the soul of the firm itself by making his outrageous claim in front of one of its employees? Do you think she told anybody else about it?

According to our Very Important Partner, and our greedy letter writer, of course, such concerns are inconsequential. Questions of morale or of treating one another with basic human respect are undoubtedly too "altruistic" for them.

But do you know what? I have a claim of my own to make. I say such people are moral paupers who live paltry lives, regardless of the nominal riches or positions they acquire. It is a delusion to think one's worth can be equated with money or title, and such delusions threaten the very fabric of our personal and public lives. Such delusions leave people like wounded animals, at once sad and dangerous.

I imagine a time in the future when such a person is dead and gone. The family has gathered for the reading of the will. Curiously, there are no tears. It seems everyone only wants to know one thing.

"What was he worth?"

Why Do We Doubt Our Noses?

IT IS A GREAT CURIOSITY that so many of us habitually assume our instinctive responses to be incorrect. We doubt our noses.

I'll give you a trivial example first. I was sitting working the other day when I started feeling chilled. My hands, especially, felt cold. It seemed everyone around me had been getting sick lately, and I was fretting about the possibility that I was coming down with something when I realized I had forgotten to close my office window the night before. The reason I was cold was because it *was* cold.

Another example, as far from trivial as you can get. A woman tells me she is afraid of her husband, afraid he might hit her. In her next breath, though, she tries to take back the truth just spoken by saying she is "sure he could never do it." Later, she offhandedly says that the hair on the back of her neck rises when he comes into the room. What other creature would doubt that message?

Returning veterans of foreign wars report widespread illness. Officials say no evidence of any environmental agents exists and attributes much of this illness to psychological problems. Later, new evidence emerges that the veterans were right all along.

A man of forty-five complains of a listless, dull feeling and worries he might be getting depressed. He doesn't know why he can't snap himself out of it. He proclaims a life that by general standards is a good and successful one. Still, he reports a deep longing. Maybe Prozac, he suggests.

I could go on for days. The move is unmistakable: actual experience is introverted. Sensations and perceptions are assumed to be projections from the subjective inner self, the inner self who says, in the first instance, "I am cold" instead of "It is cold."

This move is especially clear with regard to psychological symptoms, which we usually assume to emanate from and relate to the individual person. If we are having trouble coping with our work environment, we assume there is something wrong with our attitude, that perhaps we need to be more flexible and adaptive. If we find ourselves constantly troubled and angry, we assume the cause must lie in some kind of past personal abuse or trauma. The answer, we assume, must be within us.

But we never seem to assume that our experiences and what we call our symptoms might be correct. We never seem to ask what kind of work environment it must be for ugly words such as "coping" to be operative. We never seem to assume that if we are troubled and angry then maybe things are troubling and angering.

I'd be the last person to deny the relevance of personal experience to psychological life, but there is a great danger in assuming that all of our experiences are only personal. The danger lies in the simple fact that this excessive introversion loses the world. This was the famous move of Descartes—"I think therefore I am." In that one stroke, he sundered human from world and locked the soul in the frail shell of mortal consciousness. Ignored in his dictum is the already present fact of Descartes himself, who was hungry or not, tired or energetic, sitting in a warm room or maybe walking around town when he arrived at his great "therefore." All philosophical thought aside, there was already a there there. It is this animal presence that I am encouraging us to trust more fully.

It is an old and recurring fantasy of humans that other, so-called "lower" animals are more environmentally attuned than we are. Although we assume ourselves to have superior cognitive and motor skills, we believe other animals to possess keener senses that connect them more directly to their natural habitat.

That may be. But wouldn't it be more reasonable to assume that we, too, have an extended range of instinctive sensitivities?

This is hardly academic. Again and again in therapy I see people who are not suffering as much from their stated symptom ("I feel depressed") as they are from their belief that they shouldn't feel the symptom. Their suffering often is exacerbated by the outrageous demands erected and enforced by modern manic culture. In short, their symptoms are signs pointing not only inward into their personal consciousness but outward into the world of action and experience.

The fact is that this entire inner/outer talk is off base. Descartes was simply mistaken. If we are honest with ourselves we will admit that the world does not really seem dead to us. We will admit that many of the things that bother us are in fact bothersome. This means that our symptoms can be read as testaments to our endless connections with the world, and as providing trustworthy information about that world.

Perhaps it is an old pair of work gloves. Over the years you've sewn them up when they came unraveled because you couldn't bear throwing them away. If you lay them down their fingers reach up like they want to shake hands. Maybe you wore them to plant that tree in the front yard when your youngest was born—and just look how straight and tall now. You love those gloves, and I am asking us to make room for the possibility that the gloves make this love possible. It is not our human projections that animate the world. The world is already animated, already full of soul. It is as if the things of the world respond to us at the same time we reach out to them, hand in glove.

Can we do it? Can we rescue our trust in our animal selves? If we feel uneasy or distressed, could it be we are on to something? Could it be we are having a legitimate response to the state of things? This seems as likely to me as assuming we are the ones with a problem.

A Serious Mistake

FOR YEARS I have operated under the general rule that if someone says they are depressed then things must be depressing. Modern orthodox psychology would almost invariably place this depressive something within the confines of the person's skull and skin. According to this view, if it feels personal it must be personal, and so much time is spent investigating the person's past, relationships with parents, family setting, etc. Or, increasingly likely nowadays, the depression is assigned the status of a disease and drugged into abeyance.

This discussion is especially serious for lawyers. Surveys indicate that roughly one in four lawyers suffers from depression, compared to an overall rate of depression in the general population of 3 to 9 percent. Following my usual view, I have been assuming that this means something about the law as currently imagined must therefore be depressing. And indeed there are plenty of things to point to as evidence for this view. The reduction of a fine profession to a pack of lean, mean, legally trained entrepreneurs who think of the law as a product to be sold is alone enough to push me into the doldrums, and this is but one of many problems facing the law.

Over the years, I also have suggested that the law's depression might be related to its particular mind set. Again, there is much evidence for this view. Lawyers are in many ways trained into isolation. We are taught that maybe we are a little bit better than the lay public. Our minds are taught to approach relationships as potentially troublesome or worse.

We are schooled in the habits of worry, always concerned about what might go wrong, and so spend much time trying to figure out ways to foresee and forestall trouble. We are taught never to admit error because we must be wed to whatever argument we are making. And so on. These and many other traits that go along with "being a lawyer" do indeed distance the lawyer from just about everything else in his or her world. People around us say we are obnoxious and arrogant, and so naturally we begin to feel abandoned and cruelly misunderstood. The more we draw back from the world ("drawing back" is the etymological meaning of "abstraction") the more disinterested we become in anything but our personal territory. And the more depression becomes our partner.

But here is where I've been seriously mistaken. I still think what I have just said is true, but all along I have been holding out hope of fixing things, and this hope has derailed my efforts to engage the law's depression fairly. I thought that if the connections between the lawyer's view of the world and his or her depression could be articulated, then the depression would go away. In short, my view has been unconsciously orthodox, thoroughly American, thoroughly in keeping with modern psychology's narcissism, and thoroughly approved of by my lawyerly self. All because I have persisted in the view that law can be cured of what ails it. In this, I now think, I was completely wrong.

Nothing can happen psychologically if we approach things with an eye toward getting rid of them. The psychological fact is that whatever is there is what the soul has provided, that whatever is present is necessary and whatever is necessary is present. So if depression is prevalent in the law, then we must stay with that fact. To assume that this depression points to correctable problems, which has been my mistake, pre-judges the soul's chosen expressions by declaring them in need of adjustment. But seen without this moralistic overlay, the law's depression appears as a necessary component of the law itself. Indeed it makes as much sense to talk about depression's problems with law as about law's problems with depression. From the perspective of depression, after all, one might wonder about those three-in-four lawyers who are not depressed. How odd.

So instead of thinking about how to get rid of the law's depression, I think we must instead acknowledge it and learn to accommodate it through our legal theories and practices. I am quite aware that this flies in the face of: 1) America's delusions of innocence, 2) orthodox psychology's self-help crusade, and 3) the law's fix-it mentality. But taken together, these three strands reduce actual psychological life to pathology through the simple, though huge, mistake of thinking that whatever is wrong can be fixed. Well, whatever is wrong cannot be fixed. There is tragedy in this world and in every life; it is as natural and unavoidable as our next breath and our last.

There is great relief in realizing that we cannot fix all things to our liking. Yes, your father was never there and your mother drank too much—now, what to do? Do you remain fixated on what hurts, trying your best to make it go away? Or do you learn to do what you ultimately will have to do anyway, to live with the hurt, taking time to provide for it, to favor its needs the way a person who lives with pain comes to make small, continuous accommodations to that which inexorably is?

Lest you charge me with giving up, please note that this charge emanates from a moralistic view that already assumes too much. We simply do not know what the law's depression signifies, much less whether it can, or should, be cured. We do not know what the soul has in store for us, and we can cause much undue pain by struggling to undo fate, an impossible task based in hope and full of hubristic anxiety.

Besides, I am not saying to give up. I'm saying that there is much to be done. We must rework our theories and practices to reflect the actual experiences of our lives. That "theoretically speaking" has come to mean "unrealistically speaking" is an indictment of our theories, and so for both law and psychology, the work is to radically re-ground theoretical practice in the fertile soil of life itself.

A Hero's Life

LAWYERS, I THINK, feel called to do something big, something against the odds, something important, perhaps even salvific. One lawyer says she became a lawyer because it is intellectually challenging. Another lawyer says he became a lawyer to try to make the world a better place. Still another says she wants to do good in the world, to help the oppressed and ensure justice for all. Others, of course, just want to make a lot of money, rise to a corner office, and be in charge. Such big feelings cannot fairly be reduced to big egos, but must also be taken as indicating an abiding rhetoric that influences the lawyer's mind. This rhetoric speaks the voice of the hero.

We are routinely told that Law is the only thing that prevents civilization from sinking into anarchy and chaos, and lawyers feel particularly charged with ensuring that the Law retains control. The adversarial system itself demands a heroic attitude—one party versus another, lawyers as gladiators, hired guns, paid mouthpieces. The idea is that in a fierce but fair fight, the observers of the battle (judge and jury) will be able to discern the truth (which ironically is often imagined as a third position not clearly represented by either party), and justice will be done. In such a situation, the lawyer is charged with carrying the clumsy weight of a one-sided view with grace and integrity, and must do so over and over again, without flag or fail, in every case, from now on.

If on a cosmic level law brings order out of chaos, and on a societal level law holds anarchy at bay, and on a personal level law seeks to control our innately irrepressible lives, then the lawyer's heroic temperament could not be more in keeping with the archetypal demands of the law itself. Such a heroic view of the law requires heroes for the law to proceed at all. This isn't the only way to imagine the law, of course, but it does seem to be the prevailing view in today's world.

If the stories of heroes are to be believed, it isn't easy to live the life of a hero. All of us, perhaps, have the potential for sudden heroic acts, like the strolling stranger who without thinking rushes into the burning house, or the bystander on the street corner who pulls a child out of the way just in time. But to live daily with the fantasy that heroic acts are expected of you, required of you—that is a different thing altogether. The idea itself shows heroic proportions.

In classical stories of mythical heroes, the hero's amazing feats were made possible by the hero's relationship with divine powers. Mythical heroes always act under divine empowerment. Such heroes know that they are agents, not principles, and that they are dependent on divine powers; they are not, nor do they imagine themselves to be, independent figures. To meet the challenges given with heroic destiny, mythical heroes depend on divine gifts and support, and so actually are more acutely aware, perhaps heroically aware, of their dependency than most. The hero is inadequate without divine support, and so the hero's greatest courage may well lie in the hero's willingness to set forth against impossible odds while knowing he or she is completely dependent on greater powers that can be withheld at any time, without reason. Hence, while appearing to mortal eyes to act alone, the mythical hero is surrounded by invisible allies of extraordinary power.

According to this old view, the hero's task cannot be borne by the human ego alone. That is why all of the "stand alone," "don't let them see you sweat," "don't depend on anyone" crap that lawyers are routinely fed in law school and legal practice is so enormously hurtful. It encourages lawyers to have big heads, when it is only a big heart (the traditional place both of god-given courage and one's essential nature) that can support the lawyer in his or her heroic endeavors. Nowhere are lawyers taught that personal authority derives not from the force of personality but from the invisible forces that make personality possible to begin with.

To be clear, I am not espousing any religious belief. Rather I am arguing that our usual idea of the freestanding hero does not comport with the facts of psychological life. Such an idea focuses only on the human aspects of the hero, reducing the extraordinary to the ordinary, and thereby ignoring the exceptional implications of the hero's acts. And yet listen closely to what heroes say: "I don't know what came over me. I saw the flames and heard someone call for help. The next thing I knew I was running into the flames." I would take seriously phrases such as "something came over me," and "the next thing I knew." The hero is stating very precisely the autonomous feeling of heroism, the feeling that it comes from somewhere else. But our humanistic ears tune out such phrases, hearing only the self's mantra that everything must arise from my personal ability because there is nothing "over me." I am at the top, and there is no other god before me.

And yet in every heroic moment there is something inexplicable, as if some unseen hand of Fortune or Fate intervenes just in the nick of time. Why is it so hard for us to imagine in ways that honor this experience? Why must we try to make ourselves out to be the hero when millennia of myth, tradition, and literature tell us otherwise, that the power of the hero arises from the divine?

Since ancient times we have known that many of what we call psychological symptoms point to simple hubris, the mistaking of divine gifts for personal ability. Treatment requires first rectifying that underlying mistake, learning to render unto the gods that which belongs to the gods.

The Invisible Symptom

A MAN called me the other day and said he was depressed. "Depression," though, is a vacuous word until it is particularized in an image, so I asked the caller to tell me about his life in general and about his depression in particular.

He said he had been practicing law for fifteen years and was a partner in a mid-sized firm. He was married with two children, and a home in the suburbs. His home life was good, but he badly missed seeing his wife and children because he worked twelve hours a day, six days a week. When I asked why he worked so much, he said his partners, who brought in more business than he did, kept giving him work and he was afraid to turn any of it down. He said his partners expected him to keep up his double-time pace in return for "carrying him." He said that at his firm you "eat what you kill or live on leftovers."

He just laughed when I asked him what he did for enjoyment. "I come home, have a few drinks, and go to bed. Then I get up and do it all over again. Sometimes I think I'll just stay at my desk, stop eating, and work myself to death."

"Tell me something you love," I said, "an actual thing, not a person."

No answer.

"Do you like where you live?"

"It doesn't make any difference," he said. "I'm never there anyway."

"Do you do anything around the house?" I asked. "Laundry or cooking or cleaning?"

"No. My wife does that. I just bring home the bacon."

"Give me an image of what your depression is like," I said. "Tell me a story about it."

"I don't know how to do that." He was getting irritated now. "I just feel trapped."

"What kind of trap?"

"What difference does it make? I don't have any choice. I've got bills to pay. Can you help me or not?"

How would you respond to this man? I get this kind of call all the time, and almost invariably what people want is relief, the quicker the better. Increasingly, their first choices are antidepressant drugs.

But what about the truth this man's soul is telling? Depressed? Forced to work twelve hours a day by so-called partners holding a small carrot in one hand and a big stick in the other. Afraid, after fifteen years of service, that he could be booted out any day if someone younger and cheaper comes along. A home that he literally is out-of-touch with. Nothing loved, no passion for the things of the world, no beauty, no art. His life a repetition of toil, sleep, and expectations. Trapped? Yes.

If this man is living a depressing life, then his depression is not a sign of anything wrong with him. Although his depression is trying to draw his attention to an untenable style of life, his response—*and here is the pathology*—is to look for ways to fit in and go along with a lifestyle that is starving his soul. "Sometimes I think I'll just stay at my desk," he said, "stop eating, and work myself to death."

This comment about starving at his desk was the most useful thing he said because it gave an image to his suffering. What are we to make of this comment? He said it like a martyr, which accentuated his feelings of self-immolation, but with a small twist it opens other possibilities. Perhaps it suggests that the lean and mean life he is living needs to die so he might live differently. Maybe he does need to stop living on his current diet, and to starve those expectations that haunt and drive him. Or perhaps he is describing a hunger strike intended to draw attention to the inhuman demands of his desk and what it represents. Perhaps what he feels as a hopeless symptom is trying to incite him to action.

The invisible symptom behind this man's suffering is his inability to see what is actually hurting him. There is no courage in his story, no willingness to fight back against sordid economic principles that have overtaken his profession and limited his life, and death, to his desk. He does not trust his instincts or his intuitions and passively claims there is nothing he can do. Don't ask me to fix what is actually broken, he says, just give me something to make me feel better.

I couldn't give him what he wanted, and I wouldn't have even if I had been able to. The invisible symptom that has him has us all. We are unwilling to respond to what our suffering is showing us. The man who called me was suffering from a crisis of courage, not insufficient coping skills, and neither introspection nor prescriptions will ever help him. The sources of his pain are not within him but live within the broader span of a sickened world he has accepted and allowed. It is that world that suffers first. Like him, we must have the courage of our symptoms, and understand that taking a pill in response to a sick world is a faulty prescription pushed by tyrants.

I say long live our symptoms. They may be our last hope in restoring the courage we need for the battles ahead.

Sorry, But We're All Out of Control

A LAWYER called to say she has problems with control, that she is a "control freak" who always has to have control over the various parts of her life. When things begin to get out of control, as they inevitably seem to, she becomes anxious and feels lowered "self-esteem" because she is not up to the challenge. She called me with the usual expectation that a psychotherapist would be able to diagnose and fix her—an expectation that itself indicates a control fantasy. I told her that I did not know "what was wrong" nor could I offer any hope of "fixing it." But she persisted (she really wanted to get control of this control problem), and said that perhaps I could help her ease her pressure by learning how to let go.

The first thing to note in our lawyer's complaint about her attempt to control everything is that more than anything else it is the fantasy of control itself that is controlling her. Whether or not she is or is not in control is not as relevant as the fact that she is in the grips of a control fantasy. Even the payoff she wanted from me, her hope that she could learn to just let go, comes from a place that thinks it has hold of things and can unilaterally decide to let them go. The attempt to solve the problem of control, in other words, keeps one firmly and inexorably rooted in the rhetoric, mood, and behavior of control.

The interesting thing about control is that the person who thinks he or she is most in control is the person most completely out of control. The woman who called me was tormented by her attempts at control, but what was behind these attempts? I wonder if it is not the idea of control itself, the idea that we are the cause of things, that we can manipulate the present, that our wills are efficient and effective tools that can direct the flow of tomorrow. The mind imagined as a Corps of Engineers.

Once the mind becomes committed to control, the fantasy of control quickly tries to take over all aspects of the person. Such single-mindedness distorts the person in the direction of the now controlling idea of control. The person becomes high-strung, easily freaked out. The fantasy of control, when taken as literally real, is freakish, aberrational in its obsession.

The caller also provided insight into the symptoms of a mind controlled by control. Anxiety and lowered self-esteem were signs that control was not satisfied, a clue that both feelings are required by the idea of control. Control keeps us in line by filling us with expectations, which in turn leads to anxiety. Or, to be more precise, it is when control convinces us to take our expectations literally, as if they can actually be achieved, that anxiety arises. In fact, this tendency to take itself literally is what gives control its great blind spot by shrinking the world into control's idea of how things should be. Just note how often control freaks are boorish, aloof, and abstracted from what is actually going on. Anxiety is what literalism feels like, and when anxious we must recall that we are no longer living in the present. Even if control seems to nitpick everything in sight, its own sight is down the road because control's main concern is that things not get out of hand. Control literally believes that what happens now causes what happens later—belief in causality another main indicator of a mind controlled by control. Control lives to predetermine the future, a task usually left only to gods, which is perhaps why anxiety leaves us breathless and shaking, aftereffects of our super-temporal flight.

"Self-esteem" is more tricky because it brings with it all the defenses of the Self, an idea (yes, "self" is an idea, a theory—no one has ever seen one) that is closely allied with the idea of control. Both the self and control tend to be holistic, wanting to take everything in under one roof. Both favor a guiding voice over choruses of alternative views. Both like ideas such as "getting it together," or "being centered." Both are easily addicted to power. And both depend on highly questionable views of identity and individualism. All told, self-esteem is about as hopeless an idea as I've come across in psychology. When controlled by this reductive, narcissistic, and arrogant idea of the self and its self-control, the mind labors under the whips of masked moralisms, condemned to the dark mines of the self, forever working on finding the gold of esteem.

So I am left just where I told my caller I would be, without a clue about how she should get rid of her control problems. It seems to me that even calling it a problem reinforces the rhetoric of control. My suggestion was to inquire further into the things that her control fantasy is using to keep her under control. What does it mean to be a perfect mother, a perfect lawyer, a perfect wife (all of which were required by the control fantasy that gripped my caller)? "Perfect" is about as judgmental as you can get, so what standards are being assumed and who gets to decide whether the caller is perfect enough? What imaginal figures, what ideas, what moralisms are behind the control that controls her? She fears being out of control, but isn't that what is really called for, to get out from under the ideas that whip her mind, forcing her to obey the demons of anxiety and self? If only she could lose control, where this phrase was no longer taken as referring to her and her state of mind, but to the control that holds her under its thumb.

PART TWO

A Gentle Rebellion

ORGANIZATIONS exist as a means of communal action. Their purpose, like other forms of joint action, is to make things possible that are beyond the capacity of the isolated individual. Contrary to the now tired idea that communities are the result of social contracts drawn up between freestanding independent contractors, organizations are better imagined as given with the soul's communal nature. The word "organization" itself tells us this, deriving as it does from the Greek "organon," which referred to an implement, tool, bodily organ, or musical instrument. It is akin to the Greek *ergon,* meaning "to work."

I take this to mean that organizations, like work itself, are natural activities of the soul, given with bodily life, and containing within them the power to grace our lives with forms that sing and play. A good organization is one that is well composed, like a concerto or symphony, allowing each of its many parts to contribute to a sound unattainable through a hodge-podge of competing soloists.

No wonder, then, that when our organizations suffer

from being ill-conceived or tyrannically run, or lose sight of the common good, or suffer cancerous ideas of incessant growth that the overall tone and harmony of civilized life becomes harsh and discordant. The prevailing idea that organizations are to be used solely for personal advancement and material gain do great damage to the soul, and, because we mortals are charged with the worldly task of administering (literally "caring for") these organizations, when they suffer we suffer.

The essays in this section explore the how the Law currently lives through its organizations. As was true in Part One, the psychological move is to see these organizations as aspects of ensouled, imaginative life, and to encourage a deep respect for their needs and aspirations. Organizations are not lifeless forms, but have their own spirit, their own character. The legal fantasy of the corporation as an independent entity attests to this fact (the word *corporation* itself deriving from an old word meaning "body"). To care for our organizations, then, we must realize that we are caring for a living entity existing quite apart from our personal demands. Organizational tenure implicates us in divine service, and the essays in this section address the nature of such service.

The Vision Thing

I RECENTLY READ an interview with a group of young associates who were talking about their careers. All of them were savvy commentators on how the legal profession works. They talked about the effects of age, gender, specialization, and internal firm politics on their careers—all with an air of sophistication that belied their relatively tender years. And yet after reading the article I had a lingering sense of something amiss.

I read the article again.

During a second reading I was reminded of the old mystery writer's theme of the dog that didn't bark. It wasn't what the associates were saying that was the problem, it was what they weren't saying.

Former President Bush called it "the vision thing." Where, in all of the analysis and manipulation of the legal profession in terms of their personal careers had these associates shown any vision about the profession itself? Their language was flat, dispassionate, and far too considered. There was no sense of vitality, of young blood, of grand ideas. What was most evident in their comments was the collapse of professional and social concerns into a kind of "watch out for number one" individuality. It was like they were concerned with redecorating their staterooms while the ship they were on was sinking.

I suppose such self-interest is to be expected, especially in times of economic constraint. But the psychological implications of such short-sightedness are serious. As vision shrinks, the context provided by the peripheries is lost. When I focus only on my career, the broader concerns of how my work fits into the world can be lost.

The result of such tunnel vision is a psychological attitude that leaves us feeling confined and surrounded by threatening forces. Colleagues become adversaries, family becomes a competing interest for time and loyalty, society at large becomes an army of critics. Many lawyers complain of this feeling of alienation and isolation. I even wonder if many of the problems that lawyers have with substance abuse don't reflect an attempt to free one's consciousness from just this sense of oppression.

The other important thing about what the associates said was that they were obviously scared and probably had a right to be. Does anyone disagree that the legal profession has become more competitive? Or that firm loyalty isn't what it used to be? Or that civilized relations among colleagues is suffering? Does anyone doubt the increasing use of the "bottom line" as a means of judging success?

What can be done?

While I don't think it is asking too much for young lawyers to be advocates of change, the elders also have a burden in relieving this psychological state of affairs. Yes, young lawyers must regain the courage to have ideals. But it is up to the elders to nurture this courage by providing a sense of security and openness within the profession.

By saying that the elders have to nurture the profession's young, I don't mean fixating on "associate development" or "training"—neither of which even begin to touch the issues I am talking about here. Such clichéd responses are merely part of the "law is an industry and humans are resources to be managed" school of thought. I am talking about a higher duty. It is up to the elders to show young lawyers how to take risks, how to fail, how to put society and profession before personal ambition, that human rights are too noble to be reduced to academic cost-benefit analyses, and that loyalty is more important than profit.

On the other side of the coin, I sure would like to see more agitation from the troops. It is easy for the young to say they are biding their time and waiting until they are in charge, and that they then will change things. But I think that this procrastination is symptomatic of the very disease at hand because it displaces the pressure we feel from our neglected ideals by putting them off until another day.

Like individuals, a profession suffers when it becomes too complacent. Thomas Jefferson was right about the need for a little revolution now and then. The tendency to harden and rigidify is given with the psychological underpinning of law itself, and so it is especially important for it to heed Jefferson's advice. Traditionally, revolutions have started with youth, and it may be, as some psychologists have said, that revolution is part of what it means to be young.

I hope it is clear that I am not necessarily talking about years here. "Young lawyers" and "elders" are first and foremost states of mind and are not limited by age. Everyone knows old people who are young and young people who are old. In fact, one of the peculiar side-effects of the pathology we are exploring is that young lawyers, to me at least, seem especially old nowadays. Twenty-five going on fifty.

This premature affectation of age indicates an unconscious movement within the profession. This movement uses "tradition" as a shibboleth, and also shows up in a kind of right-wing conservatism that says only the strong should survive. I see this move as anti-psychological because it unduly limits the ways in which the profession can be imagined.

There is much talk from many quarters that the legal profession is collapsing under its own weight, that it is falling apart. On the one hand, this is cause for concern. But on the other hand, so what? Isn't the legal profession based on ideas of freedom of expression that say that over time what is good and true will emerge from an honest exchange of ideas? Maybe the profession needs to fall apart. Maybe we need to see whether the powers that be are strong enough honestly to consider not being in power. If not, maybe it is time for a little revolution. In any event, it seems to me that the only way to prevent a catastrophic revolution is to provide a context where revolution can take place all the time.

Lincoln Lives

I DON'T KNOW MUCH about Abraham Lincoln. I haven't read Sandburg's biography of Lincoln, or any other biography of him for that matter. I couldn't tell you in any detail about where Lincoln stood on any of a myriad of issues. And yet what I do have is an image of Lincoln, an enduring impression left over the years like a footprint in time.

The Lincoln of my imagination takes varying forms. One is the working Lincoln, a tall, rangy young man with rolled-up sleeves. Another is the lawyer Lincoln, making his way in a sleepy little town in downstate Illinois, encouraging his colleagues to be "peace makers." And of course there is President Lincoln, a burdened man with melancholy eyes determined that the country he loved would not perish. All of these images suggest a man of respect, humility, and steadfast conviction. A man who stood for things.

Not too long ago I visited Lincoln's home in Springfield, Illinois. It was early in the morning, and there were only a few of us in the tour—a family from South Carolina with two small children, an elderly couple, and me. Walking through Lincoln's home, seeing where he played with his kids, where he slept, where he entertained visitors, I suddenly had a strong feeling of kinship with him. Walking where he once had walked, I realized that as a lawyer I was walking where he had walked. What he did then is not so far removed from what we lawyers do now. At our best we stand for the same fundamental ideals, pursue the same causes, advocate the same positions. Like him, we, too, are devoted to justice and fairness, equality and freedom. Standing there with the tour group, I felt special, even blessed, as if I had a unique connection to Lincoln's greatness not available to the others. Not that they couldn't or didn't feel the same dedication to freedom or justice, but simply that they were not lawyers. It wasn't elitism or arrogance I felt, but pride.

Pride is a hard notion for us. Some say it is a sin. But the word itself comes from roots meaning "to be worthy," which to me means pride need not be sinful so long as we realize its intrinsic challenge. Pride, if not allowed to slip over into vanity, requires us to measure up, to answer the call. That is the legacy I felt that day, the demand to be worthy, to be willing to stand for things that matter. Amidst all of the lawyer bashing directed at the legal profession, perhaps the most hurtful is the charge that lawyers don't stand for anything anymore but are only amoral tools, rudderless ships of advocacy.

I occasionally hear lawyers say they have to be uncivil to their colleagues because a client expects it. These lawyers are wrong. It is we who are the keepers of our professional flame, and although we must advocate our client's interests we may never relinquish the ideals that have made us what we are. These are hard times for the legal profession. Fragmentation, incivility, greed, and selfishness threaten to break our communal bonds. But they also can be times of great opportunity, a time to reaffirm our union, a time to answer the call.

There are many things wrong with our profession. There also are many things right. It is important, now and then, to realize the good in what we do, not to indulge in backslapping self-congratulation, but to recommit ourselves to our highest ideals. After all, joy is not inherently less profound than depression.

Walking through Lincoln's home, I watched the youngsters

in the tour puzzle over the blocks and wooden toys on display in the children's room. Even to me those toys seemed almost ancient; imagine what they looked like to the eyes of a generation raised on video games and computers. But when we all walked outside, the children started playing tag and chasing each other down the cobblestone streets. Things change and yet stay the same. It matters not whether we scrawl our passion on the back of an envelope or type it into a word processor, what matters is the content of our message and our undying commitment to make the world a better place.

Perhaps it sounds odd to talk this way, all misty-eyed and choked up. But what's wrong with a little sentiment, with basking in the light of a legacy that sends a beacon into a world still darkened by hate, injustice, and oppression? We spend so much time fretting over and defending our profession that sometimes we forget just how noble it can be. And so I ask lawyers to pause from time to time to appreciate our legacy. To remember the heroic struggle of which we are still a part, a struggle mirrored in the lives of our heroes—Jefferson, Lincoln . . . each lawyer will have his or her own list. These figures form the mythical background of our everyday practice. When we speak we might echo their words. When we act we might honor them with our work.

Someday, many years from now, the children of the children I was with in the tour will look back at what we have done. Scant few of us will make the history books, but notoriety is not essential to greatness. Wouldn't Lincoln have been great even if he had stayed in that little town, making peace? The profession we pass on ultimately will be a reflection of a thousand little things done each day, both on and off the job. If we do our best, perhaps we can in some small measure answer Lincoln's call to "strive on to finish the work we are in . . . to do all which may achieve and cherish a just and lasting peace among ourselves and with all nations."

I walked out of Lincoln's home able to see a little farther, not because I was tall, but because as a lawyer I stand on his shoulders.

Lincoln lives.

A Proposal for Taking Stock

THE OTHER DAY over dinner, my wife and I were talking about how our respective work days had gone. At one point, she said offhandedly that it was too bad there couldn't be a day set aside at work where no one could give anybody any new work to do. She said it sure would be nice to have a day just to catch her breath.

I have been thinking about what she said, and the more I think about it the better an idea it seems. Imagine. An entire day at work where nobody could give you anything new to do. I don't mean going in on the weekend, either. I mean an actual work day set aside for workers to do whatever they think needs doing. A day to let us catch our breaths.

Think of all the little things that, right this second, are nibbling away at the back of your mind. If you quiet your current preoccupations, these nagging voices remain, insistent and inconsolable. They often are the final voices you hear before sleep comes too late. Maybe it's a backlog of filing, or some letters that you've been meaning to write, or finally fixing a desk drawer that's been sticking for a year. Such nagging omissions play on our minds, never letting us feel truly settled.

Setting aside time to catch up on things is not a new idea, of course. Spring cleaning is a wonderful example. Throw open the windows, beat the rugs, air things out, clean and wax and polish until, at the end of the day, you're dead tired but feel great, and the house smells renewed with freshness, happy from our attention.

Or what about cleaning out a closet? Give those old clothes

to charity; you never wear them anymore. Make room for some new looks. This shirt here, though, you'll never get rid of. It's your favorite and it'll rot off your back before you throw it out. Wonder what's in that box back there? Remember how sharp the clothes looked when you were done, so confident in their right-faced readiness? And how organized *you* felt when you finished organizing the closet?

Part of the enjoyment we get from cleaning up like this comes from the chance it provides for taking stock, for going back over things, regathering them for another look. Turns out that box in the back of the closet contained check stubs from ten years ago. Maybe you had wondered where they were. Maybe you don't care. But at least you were made aware of their presence.

The benefits of taking stock is not lost on business. I remember the first time I helped take inventory. It was in a book store, and I remember we closed for an entire day. We all came in early and worked late, pulling books off the shelves, counting and checking and double-checking. We found books that had fallen down behind other books, books we didn't even know we had. By the end of the day, the store looked different. It looked handled, straightened up, put right. I remember that the rows of books looked almost . . . pleased.

"Inventory" comes from "invent," which originally meant "to come upon" or "find out," and certainly there is something about taking inventory that provides room for newness and creativity. Taking stock provides a sense of closure and renewal at once—not a bad feeling to have in our repertory of experiences.

But the idea of a communal catch-up day is a little different from getting a group together to take inventory. The way I imagine it, everyone would come to work as usual, but then each worker would be free to do whatever he or she chose. What I like about this part of the idea is that everyone gets to spend a quiet day in the midst of their fellow workers. Who knows? We might even come to see the work force less as a monolith and more as a community of contributors with each worker having his or her own necessary chores to perform.

By focusing on our neglected work, we also can gain hints about our own unconscious preferences. There is significance hidden in the things we put off. Why, exactly, am I avoiding making this particular phone call? Why am I so reluctant to contact this client about her case? Why am I skirting this issue? There are lessons contained in the things that we allow to accumulate. They sometimes show us where our interests truly lie.

My wife said she wanted a day where she could catch her breath. Why is our work leaving us so breathless? Why has our work become so harried? Why, at the end of a day at work, do so many people feel exhausted? Or is it the work itself that needs to catch *its* breath? Maybe we're pushing work too hard, leaving it no time or place for inspiration. Maybe we all need to take a breather.

God knows there must be a million practical reasons not to have such a catch-up day. The thought of reduced revenues alone probably is enough to give some people fits. And I suppose there are other people who might actually have a hard time getting through a day like this because their work is creating work for other people. But I still think it's a good idea. The thought of a day in which people could come to work relaxed is appealing in itself. Just think. No deadlines and no last-minute faxes.

Socrates said the unreflected life is not worth living. Surely this maxim applies equally to our work lives. Maybe that's how some people would choose to spend their catch-up day, following this ancient advice by simply ruminating about things. Couldn't we set aside just one day for such things? I can't help but think that at the end of such a day many people would go home surprisingly satisfied; tired but curiously refreshed.

Why?

FIRST SOME OBSERVATIONS drawn from several recent studies about the legal profession, then a question:

Over half of all lawyers say that the practice of law consumes too much of their lives, leaving too little for family, friends, and self.

Only one-third of lawyers say they are very satisfied with their careers.

Sixty percent of lawyers would not recommend the practice of law to their children as a career.

Over half of the lawyers believe that incivility is an increasing problem in the legal profession.

My question is, "Why?"

I don't mean "Why is the practice of law so consuming?" or "Why aren't more lawyers satisfied with their work?" or "Why has the law fallen so in the esteem of its practitioners?" or "Why are so many lawyers acting like asses?" I mean "Why are these things happening when a *clear majority* of lawyers don't want them to?" Whatever happened to majority rule, anyway?

Think about it for a second and you'll see how peculiar this situation really is. To begin with, the context in which it occurs is significant. Lawyers are trained advocates. They seldom are daunted by superior forces, and most would be willing to stand alone, if necessary, to advance their position. Lawyers understand the uses of aggression, and the technical means for channeling it effectively. They know how to be persistent, and when to be patient. In short, lawyers are worthy adversaries.

And yet, if the studies are to be believed, if lawyers are to be taken at their own word, then within the boundaries of their own profession lawyers have become uncharacteristically passive. They might bitch, yes, but they do not act to improve things.

Why?

When asked directly about this, I find that lawyers tend to be confused by the question. This, too, is significant. Many lawyers seem never to have even entertained the idea that they could actually do something about how law is practiced. A more typical approach seems to be for lawyers to resign themselves to the base aspects of the profession, to bear them like a burden, and then to get out while they're ahead. In short, lawyers become focused primarily on their self-interests (watch out for number one, cover your ass, don't rock the boat, etc.), and live their work lives with a kind of up-and-out fatalism.

You see what has happened. On the one hand, the individual lawyer is driven more into himself or herself, straining individualism to the point of distortion. Meanwhile, lawyers defend their professional passivity by trying to claim other, insurmountable forces as being responsible for the profession's problems. Currently, the two favorite goblins are the all-powerful Rainmaker who controls the lowly lawyer's life with an iron fist, and The Client who demands mean-spirited lawyering. Or maybe it's competition that's given as the source of the problem, or the manic drive to increase the bottom-line, or ageism, or whatever. The point is that a majority of lawyers apparently have found ways to displace their responsibility for their own profession.

Broad-based professional repression permeates modern legal practice and has serious psychological implications. For example, consider how clients must feel when they encounter lawyers who believe that clients want uncivilized conduct. The truth of the matter is that the vast majority of clients want lawyers who are adept at resolving conflicts creatively, preferably in a way that is least disruptive to the client's ongoing relationships. Curiously enough, this also is precisely the service that most lawyers want to provide. And yet it seems that nowadays the gap between lawyer and client could not be greater. This estrangement of the primary relationship on which legal practice is based could not be more serious. It is of fundamental concern. Nevertheless, lawyers as a group seem either unable or unwilling to acknowledge the connection between the breakdown of the lawyer-client relationship and the excessive pressure that is building up in the legal profession due to its self-imposed repressions.

Many of the psychological discomforts felt by lawyers are not, in the first instance, personal, but rather are reflections of a distressed profession. In many ways, lawyers and the legal profession are stuck in the same ships-that-pass-in-the-night syndrome that separates lawyer and client. This in spite of the fact that lawyers desperately want to embrace their profession and to renew old vows. Lawyers want broad-based release from oppressive professional ideologies, and the longer the majority remains cowed the more likely breakdown and collapse become.

It's difficult for the legal mind to acknowledge the need for radical change. *Stare decisis* is as much a state of mind as a legal doctrine. But I believe that lawyers are tired of passing the buck and are ready to act. From a psychological perspective, nothing could be more helpful or welcome than a legal profession in which its practitioners have returned home. Collegiality, loyalty, trust, friendliness, cooperation—none of these are pipe dreams. In fact, the extent to which we dismiss such necessities as ideals is a good measure of the extent to which we have fallen into our own selfishness.

There are other possibilities, I suppose. Maybe a majority of lawyers don't really give a damn about the legal profession. Maybe all of the complaining, especially among younger lawyers, about how dissatisfied they are, is really a smoke-screen. Maybe personal ambition and greed have already won. Maybe Rainmakers and Clients really are sinking the profession, leaving behind a ship not worth saving, crawling with greedy pursers ransacking the staterooms, hoping to take as much with them as possible. Maybe it really is every man and woman for himself and herself.

I hope not. I hope it's more a case of benign neglect. Surely lawyers have it in them to love the law and to attend its needs and desires. Surely when lawyers read this they will see it as a reminder of what they already know—that they truly are charged with professional responsibility, that they truly are the Law's representatives.

Restoring the Legal Imagination

The other day I was working when . . . Ow! Paper cut! My immediate response was to cuss. Then came the medical examination, the finger squeezing and sucking, and then, as quick as the cut itself, an instant of reflection.

I realized that I was working too fast, or that at least my *hands* were working faster than they safely could work. That paper cut got my attention, pulled me down from my ambitions (I was feverishly attempting to sell some writing I had done), and stopped me by drawing a little blood. It had regulated my runaway work, like those little skips our hearts take to get back in rhythm, or the stuttering half-steps we take to walk in time with others. In another time and place, I might even have wondered if some God or spirit was playing a trick on me.

After I put a Band-Aid on, I felt clumsy doing what I had been doing because I couldn't feel anything with the tip of my finger. So I started a new task. As I worked, I wondered if that had been the point of the paper cut—to get me to do this other work? It's hard to explain, but that paper cut—that one, not every one—seemed to be more than an accident. It felt like a purposeful affliction, a necessary wounding on the order of mythical woundings that reveal the inside of things.

Obviously, I am not suggesting that we go off into reveries over every paper cut . . . although that isn't necessarily such a bad idea. No, my point is that such stories demonstrate how activating imagination can encourage a deeper respect for the invisible aspects of work, the invisible aspects that are work's essence and the source of its satisfaction.

Through such work-based revelations, we can become attached to our work in unexpected ways, more aware of the mysterious undercurrents that flow imperceptibly through our lives. In the midst of common experience we can feel the swell of eternal happenings—the whisper of ancestral voices, the pleasures of simple service, the quick cut of ambition. To some extent such moments take us out of ourselves and make us aware that we are part of something else, necessary characters in an endless work-in-progress.

I could easily have dismissed the paper cut as a minor irritation. But such a response is too meager, too small to leave open opportunity for insight. We must take care not to let such responses blind us to the epiphanies present in our work.

To be open to such opportunities, we have to practice imagination regularly. Sometimes, for example, I try to imagine that what is going on around me is taking place in a short story or novel. I try to hear an unrehearsed conversation as if it had been crafted for particular effect, and to watch the precise movements of myself and others as if they had been choreographed.

Think about it for a second. When you read a story, you know that everything in the story is necessary. The better the writer, the more this is so. Every detail belongs. Everything has significance.

Suppose an author writes that a character has a car phone. We suspect that this detail means something, but we don't know what. Maybe it's a clue that will become critical later on. Or maybe it has nothing to do with the character or the plot at all, but is simply intended to help set the scene. Whatever its eventual significance, we know that the car phone is necessary to the story, that it adds something.

Now suppose one of my clients tells me he has a car phone.

Can I not approach this detail with a similar literary curiosity? What about this car phone? What does it add to the story? Does it imply that the character wants never to be out of touch, never to be alone? Is it setting up a joke? Does it imply a context of conspicuous consumerism? Who knows? Maybe other things have to happen before I can know what the car phone portends. Or maybe I'll never know for sure. In any event, by refusing to take the car phone at face value this literary approach keeps open the car phone's potentially limitless possibilities. From this perspective, all the world becomes a stage charged with mystery and drama, romance and comedy.

In the context of everyday practice, such an approach has many benefits. Most importantly, it invigorates imagination and thereby deepens psychological experience. It also sharpens our aesthetic sensibilities, improving our powers of perception and observation. A literary approach reveals dimensions of a client's story that are unavailable to more literal approaches. It takes a third eye to read between the lines, and by listening metaphorically we expand the range of our hearing.

One moral of this story is that to increase our appreciation for work we must be more open to its imaginative dimensions. If work has become problematic, perhaps our usual thinking has become too narrow and is pinching off work's imaginative resources. Or perhaps we have allowed reductive and materialistic ideologies to drain away work's vitality, depriving work of its best and fullest expression.

Whatever lessons we draw, we must remember that work is a natural activity of the soul, and so introduces us into destiny. Our work forever includes us in a lineage of practitioners and is one of the fundamental ways in which we contribute to the communal sweep of history. But history, like the devil, lies in the details. If we are to do right by our work, to honor it and our destinies, then we must begin with little things. Little things like watching for the stories within the story that swirl constantly in the backwaters of the soul. Little things like suddenly feeling the nick of time.

The Art of Making Possible

OVER THE YEARS, I've attended a number of conferences. I've been to academic conferences (including one religious studies conference which, if can you imagine, was held in New Orleans), to a conference of safety and security professionals, to many legal conferences, and to a number of conferences of psychologists and therapists.

In each setting, at some time or another, I have had the distinct feeling that these folks belonged together, that there was a certain naturalness to the gathering. It was as if the group itself had an identity that could not be reduced to the mere sum of its individual parts. It was as if the group was itself an individual.

Now I know that if you get a hundred people together to talk about the latest in biblical translation they are likely to use similar language, to have similar interests, and perhaps even share a common demeanor and temperament. But I am talking about something else—something that feels like it's prior to, perhaps even severable from, the collection of individuals. The perceptions of group identities at these conferences were always glimpse-like, as if I caught a congealing of form just before it melted away, back into the group. It was discernible, but ineffable, like watching someone draw a picture in the air.

At such times, I felt that the group identity wasn't just a reflection of a common professional language, but rather the other way around—that the identity required the language, that the identity inspired it.

Then, the other day on the radio, I heard a poet talking about his job as a poet. He said that the poet's job was to provide images that would "enable" particular experiences. Now, coming from a poet, I assume that this rather odd word was chosen with some consideration. I don't pretend to know exactly what he means by it, but I think there is a clue in what he says. I think he is providing us a way into the question of group identity.

I take the poet to mean that *experience proceeds by and through imagination.* In other words, without imagination life becomes imperceptible. If we extend this idea, then every act, thought, and desire can be seen in the first instance as an act of imagination.

Taken together, these ideas lead to the larger idea that distinguishable group identities arise not so much from commonly held interests and language but from underlying, enabling forms of imagination. Professions, then, can be seen as genres of imagination, as poetic activities having their own natural rhythms and tones. If so, then my experiences at the various conferences could be seen as indirect perceptions of their enabling imaginations.

Czech Republic President Vaclav Havel, in a speech ominously titled "How Europe Could Fail," summarized his concerns about the present European predicament by saying, "Europe today lacks an ethos; it lacks imagination, it lacks generosity, it lacks the ability to see beyond the horizon of its own particular interests." Here again is the idea that imagination is necessary for things to take shape. Moreover, in Havel's formulation we see this enabling imagination linked to a culture's sustaining values, its open-heartedness, and its capacity for selfless vision.

Who knows how far we can take all of this. Too far, probably. But doesn't it make sense to talk about a particular law firm, university, or city having an identity all its own, and that this identity reflects a deeper style of imagination? After all, why is it funny to think about a bunch of religious studies professors loose in New Orleans? From whence does the joke derive?

What if each person saw his or her life as an enabling image, a poem in the working? I like the idea that each individual's imagination allows things to happen that could not otherwise happen. I also like the idea that individuality derives in large measure from how it echoes voices from beyond its personal range. To put it succinctly, a person's individuality is dependent upon which Gods it serves.

Lawyers, and maybe even Americans in general, tend to be a bit suspicious of such talk. It rubs hard against our belief in the sanctity of the individual because it seems to grant status to an identity not derived from or based on individuals. It rubs against our sense of personal freedom because it implies that our lives might be responsible to interests beyond those of our own choosing. And it rubs against our youthful secularism by flirting with ideas about eternal, enduring Forms, thereby tinging every creation with a patina of repetition. Just when we thought we were ready for the New Millennium, we're back with Plato.

But to bring this home to the legal profession, what if each lawyer saw his or her work in terms of providing enabling imagination? After all, isn't that what lawyers do anyway? Don't lawyers provide things that make things possible? In light of the ideas we've been discussing, this activity becomes imbued with a renewed sense of artistic responsibility. Legal practice then becomes a necessary art, and the quality of a lawyer's work can be viewed, and valued, in terms of what it makes possible, what it enables.

I think we must begin to imagine our professional identities as if they have lives separate from us, interrelated with us perhaps, but not *reducible* to us. Perhaps such imagining is beyond the pale of our modern minds; perhaps we are inextricably trapped in our narcissism. Still, I cannot help but remember those conferences and the feelings they inspired. Could it be that our professional bonds are based on more than common education and training? Could it be that our professional identities are part of the very structure of things, that they are expressions of the *anima mundi,* the soul of the world?

A Note on Secretaries

SECRETARIES often complain that they and their profession are not granted the respect they deserve. Increasingly, we see the modern secretary reduced from his or her capacity as a personal assistant and aide to that of a data-entry specialist. Much is lost in this reduction, which is usually carried out as part of the current hysteria about the bottom line. Could it be that the current epidemic of repetitive stress injuries is a physical reflection of this other reduction, the reduction that takes place in our imaginations when we harden a person into only one thing? Who knows, but I do know that one way of increasing respect for something is to look again at its deeper, more essential aspects. So we might ask: what does it mean to be a secretary; what is the profession's tradition; who are the progenitors of the field; what Gods are involved?

The modern secretarial profession continues a tradition dating from the old clerical (as in church-related) ranks. During the middle ages, clerical work was provided largely by the church because that was where businessmen could find literate men who were not themselves property holders. You note that I say "men." That is because the role of clerk ("clerk" comes from the same root as "cleric") was, in these early days, traditionally a man's. Not until the middle of the nineteenth century, with the expansion of educational opportunities for women and the development of office machinery, did larger numbers of women enter the clerical field. It wasn't until 1872, for example, that the British Post Office first admitted women clerks, thereby providing the first large-scale access for women into the business world.

In 1873, another watershed event occurred in the secretarial profession, this time in terms of a technological advance coupled with a visionary marketing idea. With the public introduction of the typewriter, Remington, the original manufacturer of the typewriter, hit upon the revolutionary idea of training women to demonstrate the new machines, and the rest, as they say, is history. (At about the same time, in 1876, the Bell telephone system was founded in the United States, and it soon became a major foothold for women trying to enter the work force. By 1902, there were 37,000 women operators compared with only 2,500 men. By the turn of the century, women formed 45% of all telephonic and telegraphic employees, 29% of all government employees, and 25% of all civil service employees.) Women were still largely closed out of business, however, where clerical work was still dominated by men. But the trends were inevitable. In 1890, women held 15% of all clerical jobs in the United States. Ten years later, one-third of all office workers were women. By 1975, 99.1% of all secretaries in this country were women, and 99.2% of legal secretaries were women.

Along with this remarkable expansion of the role of women in the secretarial profession, of course, has come sexual stereotyping and abuses of power by so-called superiors. Secretaries have been called "substitute wives," and clichés about office affairs between men "bosses" and women secretaries still pervade popular views of the secretarial profession. And yet, to this day, the secretarial profession provides one of the greatest opportunities, and greatest challenges, to the achievement of equal rights for women in the workplace. This tension is part of the secretarial tradition.

This kind of historical reflection is worthwhile because it

reminds us where the modern secretarial profession comes from. By remembering that one aspect of this heritage is the profession's influential role in the expansion of equal opportunities for women, we might pause to consider if we are furthering that tradition today. Are our current ways of thinking about secretaries and secretarial work respectful of this tradition? Or is there still too much chauvinism directed toward secretaries, too much condescension and belittlement, and too little value given to their talents and capabilities? Similarly, this historical reflection might even help us to rekindle some affection and appreciation for the secretary's everyday tools. The next time we sit down in front of our sleek, modern computer, we might remember those bulky old Remingtons and the advances they made possible.

The word "secretary" itself comes from the same root as "secret," and in its earliest form "secretary" denoted a confidential assistant, a personal correspondent. We still see these old meanings today within the diplomatic corps with its Secretaries and sealed pouches, its darkly windowed limousines, and its hushed, behind closed-doors conferences. The Renaissance philosopher Marsilio Ficino said that secretaries were governed by the planet Mercury, which adds a divine parentage to the secretary's work. Mercury is the Roman form of the Greek God Hermes. You might remember him as the God with the winged shoes and helmet. According to Greek mythology, Hermes was the messenger God. He also was the unseen bringer of dreams (he would stand at the head of the sleeping person and whisper the dream into them), the mediator between warring divinities, and the only God who regularly traveled between the world of the living and the underworld of souls. Indeed, this mediating capacity was his primary divine function. His role as intermediary in no way *detracted* from his divinity, but expressed it.

If the secretarial profession has been reduced in esteem and valuation, then it might help to reconnect it to its historical and mythological sources. Through the lenses of these older views, we might once again see secretaries as the keepers of secrets, whether they be the confidential matters and correspondence that cross their desks, or the mastery of the inscrutable machines that have always been so essential to their work, or the archaic mysteries of shorthand, which to the uninitiated resembles nothing so much as automatic writing from another realm. We might recall, the next time a secretary quietly enters a meeting room to deliver a confidential missive and then drifts away behind a gently closed door, or when a secretary intervenes between warring factions or travels between worlds, that in these acts is the great Hermes, messenger of the gods, bringer of dreams.

Between a Rock and a Hard Place

I HAVE HERE a letter from a solo practitioner in Florida who wants to know whether an experience she is having is common among lawyers. She says that her state of mind seems to be directly linked to how "busy she is at work." When she has plenty to do, she often feels under a great deal of stress, but when things slow down a bit she starts getting anxious. And when things get really slow, she becomes prone to depression. She ends her letter with an extraordinary question: "Could it be that high stress keeps depression at bay?"

Remembering that there is never only one psychological response to anything, let's consider some various ideas.

First, perhaps stress does keep depression at bay. Much of what we moderns call stress is the result of a manic lifestyle—too much to do and too little time, caffeine and sugar to get us started in the morning (to sleep past noon a sinful indulgence), exhaustion or illness the only things that can stop us, playing hard and working hard, give it to me quick, and so on. Depression, in fact, is often imagined by psychologists as being in "bipolar" relationship to mania, and certainly all of us, to some degree, know the pendulum mood referred to by the phrase "manic-depressive." The big idea here is that mania and depression are connected, that they occasion one another, are in tandem. If so, then although stress might keep depression at bay, it also ensures depression, requires it. Where one goes, so goes the next.

There also is the possibility of using work as a defense against depression. Notice how the letter writer equates being "busy" with working. Could she be using busywork to defend against her depression? Maybe her real work *is* her depression. After all, the admonitions that depressed people often hear from others such as "pull yourself up by your bootstraps," or "snap out of it," or "look on the bright side," or "you should get busy," are almost always manic defenses and denigrations of depression. It never occurs to our communal mania actually to honor the depression or to consider that it has things of great value to offer us. One also has to wonder how her work must feel about being misused in this manner. Perhaps the work could benefit from depression's relative slowness and contemplative manner. Certainly one sees more while walking than while running.

According to the letter writer's account, whenever her attention is not drawn away by business (same roots as "busy"), the depression is there. It's as if the depression is always there, underneath the work. If so, then we might wonder whether the depression is actually sustaining the work, providing the moisture and deep nutrients that it needs to stay active, a view quite different from our usual prejudices that see depression as a hindrance to work.

Thirdly, we note that it is anxiety that bridges the feelings of stress and depression. Some psychologists suggest that anxiety and depression are themselves "stress inducing," but here we must be careful to distinguish our feelings. Depression certainly brings with it a sense of heaviness. In classical thought, the metal of depression was lead, then considered the heaviest of all metals. So, if we recall that stress is an engineering term, then we can see how depression's heaviness might induce stress. But this is quite different from the stress induced by anxiety. Anxiety sees through darting eyes and breathes short and shallow breaths; it is all clammy hands and adrenaline sweat. Here, stress is more a matter of *tension* than weight, as our capacities are stretched like taut muscles ready to tear and snap.

Although the letter writer didn't mention this, I would think that as a solo practitioner she also must acutely feel the pressures of supporting herself. There is a great and widespread anxiety in this country about the ever-impending threat of personal poverty and ruin. All of us are acutely aware of just how close we always are to failure—kicked out on the street, nowhere to go, no longer able to make ends meet. Fear of losing one's livelihood and security has seldom been greater, and this fear has enormous psychological power. Surely it lies at the root of the national disgraces of the homeless, the poor, and the hungry. Surely all of us can see ourselves in the eyes of the bag-person, and choose for precisely that reason to look away.

But in light of what we have been considering, we have to be careful not to allow such fears to obscure what the soul is telling us. It may well be our work that "supports" us, providing our "means of support," but if we are true to the letter writer's story then we must keep open the possibility that it is depression that supports the work.

Here we find a possible way through the vicious cycle of stress-anxiety-depression. What if we were to invite depression in instead of using work-induced stress as a means of keeping it at bay? It's going to come in eventually anyway, so why not as an invited guest instead of a surprise visitor? What if we made more room in our everyday lives for depression, collapse, and failure—all things that are as much a part of life as elation, standing tall, and success? Especially with regard to work itself, what if we were to moderate our competitive self-interest so as to find a place for depression? Our work could benefit greatly from our depressive talents. For example, the insights that come while sitting quietly with something for a long time, leaden of limb and heavy with contemplation, are unavailable to us while on our manic flights, and are but one of depression's many gifts. Such truths are difficult to keep in mind when caught in the bustle of our communal mania, but we really should give depression the respect it is due.

Tocqueville's Letter

IN JULY, 1827, six days before his 22nd birthday, Alexis de Tocqueville wrote a letter to his life-long friend, Louis de Kergorlay. Four years later, Tocqueville would travel to America, ostensibly to study the American penitentiary system but in fact to study American democracy. With his friend and traveling companion, Gustave de Beaumont, Tocqueville traveled as far west as Lake Michigan, and as far south as New Orleans. Then, four years later, in 1835, he published volume one of *Democracy in America*. The rest, as they say, is history.

But about that letter to Kergorlay. At the time, Tocqueville was finishing his law studies and was writing to his good friend about the experience of learning the law. It is an exceptional letter, especially for someone of such tender years. In it, Tocqueville wrote:

> I am beginning to think that I will adopt the spirit of my profession . . . I am concentrating on it so much, I am living outside of all society and of all affections of the heart, that I am beginning to fear that I will become a law machine like most of my fellows, specialized people if ever there were any . . . I would rather burn my books than reach that point! Who however can foresee the effects of daily influence, and who can say that he will not submit to the common rule? The second fear is that by dint of proceeding [toward] . . . a goal, I would see only that in life, that this ambition . . . would take hold of me completely, absorbing all

> other passions, and if, as is only too possible, this ambition could be satisfied, it would make me miserable.

How little some things change over the years. Then, as now, there was something at work in the "spirit of the profession" that tended to make its practitioners feel outside society, set apart from daily life, and somehow lacking in affections of the heart. Tocqueville points to the peculiar kind of "concentration" that the law requires, and recognizes the danger of allowing the law to absorb all other passions. He also is alert to the life-draining potential of goal-oriented thinking and personal ambition, and, remarkable for a man of his age, he sees that by proceeding on such a course he eventually would find only misery.

Compare Tocqueville's comments with today's leading psychological complaints among lawyers that they feel inadequate and inferior in interpersonal relationships, that they feel isolated and alienated from society at large, and that they feel that legal practice has become all-consuming, leaving little or no time for loved ones or even themselves. The correlation is too close to be mere coincidence. Apparently there was, and is, something innate in the structure of the law's imagination that gives rise to such concerns, something that crosses freely over abstract political demarcations and differing systems of justice. Whatever this something is, it appears to be part and parcel of the legal imagination itself, something that runs parallel to various legal systems but is not coterminous with them, something that perhaps is even their ground.

Tocqueville's comment about his fear of becoming "a law machine" also rings familiar to modern ears. How many times must we hear lawyers talk about feeling "fungible" or that they are only parts in a profit-generating machine before we begin to take such comments seriously? Of course, the folks who own and run the machine, and who reap its main rewards, will pooh-pooh such talk and instead preach about increasing productivity, re-engineering for maximized efficiency, and so on, but such talk is to be expected and should be seen for what it is. Significant changes and reforms rarely come from the top. But if, as appears to be the case in both Tocqueville's time and our own, lawyers allow themselves to be bamboozled into imagining life and work in terms of machines and engineering, then we should not be surprised that stress continues to build as our mechanistic fantasies take hold.

Possessed with an almost preternatural political savvy, Tocqueville also was able to see how such a transformation into a law machine actually takes place. It isn't overt tyranny that severs the bonds of society and overthrows affections of the heart, but "the effects of daily influence." It is "with time" that he fears he will become a law machine. Applied to everyday life, it is the daily drain of living in a home that feels like a hotel, eating food that one doesn't remember, sharing life with loved ones who say we seem distant, going through the predetermined and professionally sanctioned motions and habits of thought that allow us to fit in, go along, and be part of the team. It is seeing work as a necessary evil, done only to fulfill economic needs. It is allowing personal worth to be replaced by the bottom line. It is slowly, ever-so-slowly, growing more reticent, more uncertain, more quiet. Meanwhile we ignore the symptoms that are all around us, asking for our attention, trying to move us to action, trying to get us to offer just a little resistance. That is how freedom is lost, through the steady erosion of countless assaults on the soul, a little bit of integrity lost here, a little bit of love washed away forever there.

How could one so young know so much? Well, there was the gift of genius, of course. But I suspect that many lawyers know inside what Tocqueville wrote about so eloquently. The law can be a beautiful thing when it remains connected to the ongoing life of the world, but it becomes hardened and dangerous when exiled within itself. So let us escape the camp of concentration and remember that neither we nor the law can live well without the pleasures of society, the warmth of our passions, and the abiding affections of the heart.

The Fantasy of the Billable Hour

THIS IS NOT going to be a diatribe on the shortcomings of the billable hour. Anyone who has sold their services on an hourly basis knows about the dehumanizing effect of reducing one's life to a ledger entry. What I am interested in is the fantasy of work that is implied by the billable hour. This is a basic move for psychological reflection. If we look at everyday life as a *poetic field,* then the things within this field can be seen as having imaginal significance. Every move, every thought, every fantasy then becomes an opportunity for soul-making by allowing us to complement (not *replace*) our usual literal perspectives with deeper, metaphorical reflections. The psychological perspective considers all things first in terms of their significance for the psyche, or soul.

One way into this soul-based perspective is to ask simple questions. For example, exactly how does a worker who bills by the hour know when he or she is working? I mean, if you're digging ditches and have a supervisor watching you, it's pretty straightforward. But lawyers for the most part do their work behind closed doors, at least metaphorically speaking. There are the obvious results, the "work-product" we call it, but the actual creative, lawyering process is an invisible one. Especially to the client.

It was clients, after all, who originally wanted the billable hour. Before its advent, lawyer bills were more along the lines of "For Professional Services: $XXX." The billable hour was an attempt by the client, not only to rein in legal fees, but to gain insight into the legal process. "What exactly are you doing?" is the question they wanted answered.

Well, the basic problem is that it is impossible to quantify intellectual work. Non-lawyers scoff about lawyers billing time while they're in the bathroom, but if we are actually honest about the nature of work we must acknowledge that work goes on in stranger places than the john.

Take an example from a non-legal but analogous process. I'm at my desk writing. Some of the time I'm literally writing, typing words into my computer. Sometimes I'm staring out my window. Sometimes I can't get things to move, so I get up and make a pot of coffee, or run to the store, or whatever. Perhaps when I come back, I find that what was unclear before can be seen through now, perhaps not. Maybe I grow depressed and call a friend, or am distracted by some errant idea.

When, exactly, am I working? It seems to me that all of it is work. It seems to me that the coffee making and distractions are part of the work, that it all goes into the hopper. Perhaps the friend I call will move my emotions, or grant me an insight, or tell me a joke that will find its way into the work. Who knows?

Transferred to the world of the billable hour, which of these activities could, in your mind, properly be "billed"? The point, not to belabor it, is that the billable hour is not now, never has been, and never will be an actual measure of the lawyer's work. I mean this literally: you cannot accurately quantify what lawyers do. There are plenty of everyday examples of this. The fact that partners write off time they consider excessive, or that we adjust fees to please clients, or that haggling occurs over court-awarded attorney fees all points to the ambiguous nature of the creative process. Lawyers know that they cannot actually reduce their work to blocks of time, and yet by persisting in the illusion that they *can* they risk fueling the very cynicism in their clients that they wish to avoid.

Most lawyers probably would count my "desk time" as properly billable. Fair enough, but one problem with this is that over a period of time we begin to believe this compromise. Then we begin to feel that the only time we are working is when we are at our desks being productive. But to confuse work with productivity is an insidious error. So-called "downtime" is every bit as necessary for work to proceed as is having your nose to the grindstone. When we forget this, work becomes necessarily manic and compulsive—no time to stop, got to keep at it, I'll never get this all done in time.

None of this means that we should do away with the billable hour (although maybe we could be more open to alternatives). The important thing to keep in mind is that the billable hour is a fantasy, a fiction that we use as a rough approximation for measuring the lawyering process in terms of an *economic* construct. Everyone knows that you cannot encapsulate creativity and intellectual insight, and as long as we remember this going in we're O.K. But we lose our way when we begin to take the billable hour literally.

I often tell clients that one reason I charge what I do is because, from that moment on, they are going to be alive in my imagination. Perhaps I will think of one of them while I'm making dinner, stirring the dreams they have told me into my stew. Perhaps it will be in bed late at night when I will take up their case, peering into darkened corners for ideas and images that might serve the soul, waiting, with them, for the sun to rise. How does one reduce such work to a *number*? No less is true for the lawyer's work.

On this last point, allow me the diatribe that I suppressed at the beginning. The billable hour is a concept, a number, a mathematical abstraction. *It is not real.* Debates rage over when life begins, and some say we cannot be sure when, or even if, it ends. With such fundamental issues left unresolved, we might take our hourglass fantasies of work with a grain of salt, or should I say sand.

The Past Is Not Dead

AS THE LAW has become increasingly caught in the grip of economic concerns about competition and the bottom line, there has been a growing disrespect for those at both ends of the legal profession's continuum. Younger lawyers are more and more treated like impersonal profit-generating centers while older lawyers, whose productivity when measured in quantitative terms *must* decrease, are being cast off in shameful ways. In essence, we have an attack on both ends at once by those in the middle who would deny their necessity, all in the name of an almost machine-like efficiency. The result is a deadening of the soul at its deepest levels.

The law desperately needs the ambition and inspiration of its young lawyers, but is losing them to obsessive concerns with self-advancement and personal gain, all because they do not feel a sense of being held and protected by their elders. Studies suggest that very few young lawyers feel they have an older lawyer to whom they can turn as mentor. And I am not talking about inheriting clients, either, but rather the critical importance for a young person to be perceived by and—dare I say it—loved by an older person.

Our elders are suffering a similar fate. We increasingly see our profession torn by an attitude that seems to say "I'm going to get mine and then get out because no one will look after me later." The very people who could provide the depth of experience and patience that young lawyers so desperately need are being expelled by the profession in its manic drive for increased profit. Although it is more usual for us to talk about the need of the young for the advice and guidance of the old, we often forget that few things are more important as we grow older than to be held in the hearts and affections of our juniors. If we allow such abuse at both ends of the career path, our time on the road will be fraught with residual bitterness, anxiety, fear, and loneliness. Up or out is no way to live.

One way through this impasse is to ask whether what we feel as intergenerational tensions really have to do only with us. Or is it possible that these tensions really point to a breakdown between us and the timeless parade of generations themselves? If we are having trouble with one another, might we turn instead to our mutual obligations to those generations many times removed from our current affairs?

I am suggesting that the legal profession must expand and deepen what has become a dangerously narrow and constrained imagination. In other times and cultures, the living generations found common ground in their joint worship of the ancestors. The idea was that the ancestors never really leave, but remain present to influence the world of the living. Nor were these ancestors reduced only to literal family ties or blood kin—the ancestors included the tutelary spirits, gods, and demons that comprised a broader world of essential interactions. In Roman thought, the ancestors provided the *genius* or constitutive vision of a family, a city, or an occupation. The invisible ancestors made possible current endeavors.

But who speaks today of the ancestors? Who among us knows and consciously honors the history of our law firms and legal institutions? Who among us has heroes drawn from the law's past, and do we strive to measure our work by their great deeds? Who among us feels the eternal presence of the law's legacy?

No individual or group can be fully alive without honoring the guardians of the past. Indeed, we might recall Faulkner's comment that the past isn't dead, it isn't even past. Whom do we honor, or discredit, by our current conduct? What would the great and founding figures of our profession say about what we are doing? When the ancestral councils are held, do they rejoice, or weep, at what we have become?

I don't know the answer to these questions. But I do know that without such guidance we can never hope to have a sense of purpose or direction. Cut off from our ancestral imaginations we can do nothing but act blindly, repeating a history never known, much less forgotten. We will continue to seek instant gratifications in a desperate and doomed attempt to find true satisfaction, a satisfaction that can be achieved only when we once again are held in the arms of the ancestors. We living need one another, yes, but we alone are not sufficient.

Allow me a quiet challenge. As we confront the conflicts that hold us apart, can we feel the presence of those ancestral bonds that hold us together? When we decide to get rid of a senior lawyer because he or she no longer produces at the levels mandated by our economic fictions, can we stop to consider the effect of our decision on the law's legacy? What might our grandparents and great-grandparents say about such behavior? When we deride young lawyers for being selfish and greedy, can we see that we elders have created a world that encourages these vices? And when, in our youthful exuberance, we proclaim a brave new world, can we remember that such a proclamation is itself as old as time, and ensure a place of honor within it for those who have gone before? Can we begin again to hear the voices of the ages? Of all groups within our society, should it not be we lawyers who begin this gentle rebellion?

We all know we are supposed to be aggressive and ambitious, but is there not also room for humility? Or have we become so obsessed with looking out for number one that we have forgotten the countless others such a view necessarily excludes?

So I call upon old and young alike to honor our profession by honoring those invisibles who are watching. They wish us well, but they cannot help us unless or until we ask.

What a Law Degree Can Do With You

OVER THE YEARS, we all have heard someone say that there are many things one can do with a law degree. Perhaps it was someone in law school who never seemed quite sure of why he or she was *in* law school. They would sigh, and say there were bound to be lots of things to do with a law degree. Or perhaps it is someone we know now who, after practicing law for a while, has moved on to other things, and yet still remarks on how often the law seems to come up.

It is certainly true that you can do a lot of things with a law degree, but I want to be careful about this question of "doing." It is a peculiarly American trait to ask so insistently what we can do with something. An idea comes up, or we find an odd piece of metal, or we stumble across a new theory and we immediately demand "What can we do with it?" The problem, especially in the realm of ideas, is that this move can kill a young idea with pragmatic demands that are beyond its limited life experience. Too many ideas die in infancy in America from premature exposure to the rigors of doing.

So I am reluctant to say there are many things you can do with a law degree even though I know it to be so. Somehow I find it too . . . small to talk about the law in that fashion. I know we mean such comments as praise, but I can't help but hear them as reductive. I want to hold the law as something precious, something valued for more than its instrumental value alone. I want a law degree to be a testament to a refined aesthetic that opens the eye of the holder to behold the world anew. I want to say it is one thing to know about the law and another to become a lawyer, which I take to be a state of being and not only doing. I want being a lawyer to *mean something,* and I fear we slight the law when we focus too much on practical applications, as if one studies the law simply for something to do.

What is curious in all of this is that we should find it surprising or even noteworthy that the law applies so broadly in the first place. Our surprise is perhaps an indication of what has happened to the law in modern times, namely the compartmentalizing of an instinctual activity into a narrowly defined (and confined) profession. But the law has never been limited to traditional legal practice. The law is located in life itself. The law really is in those case books, really is common law. It is therefore a subtle mistake even to speak of applying the law to the facts. Why? Because the law is already in the facts.

This leads to a nice thought. Imagine a lawyer who used to practice law but has now turned to another endeavor. Let's say she has become a choreographer. To her surprise, she finds that even after years away from legal practice she still often calls on her old expertise. We could take this as an example of the many things you can do with a law degree. But we could also imagine that the reason she is able to see the legal aspects of her new life is because the law was already there to begin with. We could imagine that the law, that peculiar civilizing instinct, is already everywhere, latent in life. No, not latent but manifest, the law inscribed on life itself, readable to eyes trained to recognize it. "Reading the law" would then become the perfect path for the lawyer, but not a reading confined to books alone. To the legal eye, the handwriting is everywhere. And the more the lawyer reads, the more he or she finds in the text. Life and law begin to echo with old ideas, the way Plato said that all knowledge is a remembering.

But with knowledge comes responsibility. Imagine our choreographer in a meeting with the dance company. A difficult question arises. Perhaps there is a problem between two of the dancers, or perhaps it is a money affair, or perhaps an ethical dilemma has reared its horned head. The company turns to the choreographer. She is a lawyer, after all, and lawyers are supposed to know about such things.

Maybe at first she balks. The company's financial officer is at the meeting, as are two of the company's largest donors. Surely these people have more to say about such matters. I'm a choreographer, she thinks. But the eyes of the company are on her, and she sees that even those people to whom she herself might have turned for advice are also looking to her for help.

And so she does what lawyers have always done, and, the Gods willing, will always do. She stands to speak. Not the speech of personal preference or ideology, but the blindfolded speech of one trying to be honest, fair, and decent. She knows she does not speak only for herself, but also for every lawyer who ever strove to do right by the law.

All of which suggests that we might refine this question of doing. We might ask not what can we do with a law degree, but what can a law degree do with us? If I am right that the law inheres in the infinite forms of life, then by definition there are limitless opportunities to serve the law wherever it lives.

And so the dance company meeting adjourns and everyone heads back to work. The issue is not resolved, but it has moved, and the choreographer is glad to have been of service.

She muses that maybe choreography and law are not so far apart after all, and as she walks out of the room with her colleagues and goes back to being mostly a choreographer, she moves from Bar to barre with a grace people have come to expect in her.

Where Does the Client End?

WHO, OR WHAT, is a client, and where does the client end? Is it only the person on the other end of the phone or across the desk? If that person is acting as an officer or director of a corporation, is the client only the corporation as an abstract entity? What defines a person or a corporation, anyway?

The immediate reason for such questions is that most lawyers agree that a lawyer's primary duty is to represent the client. The rules by which lawyers practice even codify this responsibility. If so, then it behooves us to know what we are talking about when we use the word *client.* Otherwise we risk losing avenues of service to the client because our vision of the client is too narrow and exclusive.

Another reason to enquire further into the limits and definitions of *client* is more overtly therapeutic. Studies suggest that lawyers experience high levels of loneliness and a persistent sense of social isolation. If so, then it makes sense to look at what most lawyers take to be the primary relationship in a lawyer's professional life, that between lawyer and client. Could it be that the lawyer's sense of isolation is in part due to an overly restrictive view of the client?

The oldest meaning of *client* comes from Latin, and was literally "one who is at another's call." The word *client* itself derives from word forms meaning "hear" or "listen." The pecuniary connotation so common today did not come into play until later, when *client* took on its more familiar meaning of "customer."

This little history raises a nice question. One current mantra in the legal profession is client service. Much is said about the importance of listening to the client, of rapidly serving the client's needs, fax for fax, and of understanding the client's business and particular requirements. When it comes time to give advice, the lawyer is to be succinct (what with the clock running, and all), and suitably entrepreneurial. Today's lawyer is supposed to do his or her best to speak the client's language, censoring as much legalese as possible, all in an attempt to fit into the client's needs.

But our word history suggests that the primary listening responsibility belongs with the client. The client comes to be heard, yes, but primarily to listen. The lawyer's primary responsibility, then, is to speak well. But here our opening concern resurfaces: how can I speak well to the client if I don't know who or what I am addressing?

Perhaps one way to approach this question is to imagine a particular need or decision in your own life. Let's say you need to have your house painted. Simple enough, right? Now begin to imagine the range of considerations that go into such a nominally mundane decision. You begin to look for painters. You ask friends and family for recommendations. Perhaps you see a sign down the street where another house is being painted and make a note to call that outfit. The colors themselves require much attention. Some are too bright, or too out of place with the rest of the neighborhood. The house itself seems to give clues as to proper shade and hue. Maybe you've always liked green, and have a memory of a particular green that you wished you could match. And so on.

The point is that no decision is self-contained or has only personal ramifications. Every decision immediately takes us out of ourselves, and, like people themselves, are inherently pluralistic and worldly based. In fact, every action we take throughout the day reaches beyond ourselves into the larger world. Plumbing connects us to the subterranean and watery worlds beyond our vision and smell, the light switch on the wall plugs us into an international grid, the bread we eat carries not only the ingredients listed on the package, but the invisible traces of its origins, and, if it's good bread, the hands that made it. Meanwhile, electron microscopes reveal that we are never alone, but share the world with a range of life beyond our wildest conceptions.

This blurring of individual lines is not only technical or materialistic. Maybe you decided to use a certain painting contractor as a means of appeasing an in-law. Or maybe you chose a certain paint brand because of the company's environmental sensibilities. Whatever the consideration, we see that every decision reaches outward and beyond, like a dropped pebble sending ripples across a pond.

So where does the client end? If the client's job is to listen to the lawyer's call, then already the client is expanded merely by taking part in the lawyer's calling to do right by Justice. This means the client now extends also into the lawyer's world, that client and lawyer share a common space. It is the lawyer's job, then, to articulate this new world for the client, and to show the client how this world already exists invisibly interwoven in the client's existing situation. That would suggest, would it not, that the lawyer would address as many aspects of the client's given context as possible? *If the lawyer's imagination of the client stops short, then the client cannot fully be served.*

"Can I break this contract?" asks the client, and then waits to hear. The lawyer could take this question as a technical one, and focus strictly on the technicalities. Or the lawyer might also speak to the client of social responsibilities, of the importance of keeping one's word in a civilized world, of the school of hard knocks that says sometimes you live with a raw deal, or of the future ramifications of actions taken now.

So, as usual, I can't answer my own question. I don't know where the client ends. My preference, of course, is to leave things ambiguous because that is how they appear. But I do know that, however we define the client, the lines we draw will demark the limits of our service.

Why Do Things Look the Same?

IT GOES WITHOUT SAYING that today's law firms are doing their best to emulate corporate financial practices. All around the country, law firms are striving to maximize the bottom line so as to ensure the maximum income for their shareholders, who are assumed to be the partners of the firm. Indeed, more and more law firms are turning over law firm economics to people expert in the corporate style of finance. Look at the average worker in a law firm and you will see a mirror image of the average worker in corporate America—overworked, underpaid, angry at management, and terrified to do anything about it because, as management makes clear in its bottom line to labor: "You're lucky to have a job at all."

There is little doubt that the economic situation in America is antithetical to soulful life. I don't know if there is something intrinsic to free market capitalism that leads to this soul-suffering, but I do know that our current economic views are having precisely this effect. Even millionaires say they are afraid of being *homeless.* In the mind of our economic theories, there is no middle ground—either rich or on the street—and the absence of this middle ground directly indicates a loss of soul, which traditionally has occupied the middle of all things.

I intend to ride this horse for quite a while. The duty of a psychologist, after all, is to make all things more psychological, more soulful, more attendant to the mystery inherent in life itself, a mystery intimated by that wonderful and strange old word—"psyche." So when cultural events manifest in a manner that is hurtful to the soul, it is the psychologist's job to resist. And by this I mean the psychologist in each of us.

Turning a psychological eye on economics is a daunting task, what with all those smartly dressed people with their computer programs and smug projections. Burgeoning competition, they will say, justifies the need to be lean and mean in a dog-eat-dog world. Perhaps, but my question is more basic. I want to know why we are letting economic theories run our lives. I want to know how a tool has become the master. I want to know why everyone is too busy to enjoy the simple pleasures of everyday life. And I want to know why we perpetuate economic theories that make us mean, insecure, greedy, and crazed.

My hunch is that we are living according to a manic idea run amok. Consider. Why, exactly, do I have to make more money next year than this? Why, if I already have enough, do I have to get all I possibly can? As Jake Gittes asked the rich and terrible Noah Cross in the movie *Chinatown* about a heartless scheme for money and power: "Why are you doing it? How much better can you eat? What can you buy that you can't already afford?" Computer projections are incapable of considering such outrageous questions. You must get more, says their artificial intelligence, because that's the program.

But let us be clear. Nothing in our world grows the way the free marketeers insist that the economy grows. Please hear the lesson of over two thousand years of psychological investigation: *The untempered drive to acquire for the sake of acquisition is a manic desire that must end in collapse and depression.* Have you noticed how little time there is for reflection? Mania is incapable of self-reflection. That's why it's manic.

But my question is a simple one. Why do law firms look increasingly like corporations? It seems to me that an organization run by people who have declared their allegiance and divine servitude to Justice would look different from other organizations. You would expect such an organization to be a leader in finding ways to actualize the Law's greatest ideals in the workplace. You would expect such an organization to have employees fully confident that those in charge are trying to do the right, just, and fair thing. There would be much charity. People would know that their voices are heard, heeded, and even needed. Such an organization would be both flexible and stable, like the Law itself, and everywhere, in every department, the image of Justice would beam her light through the procedures and processes by which the organization conducted its affairs. Everywhere would be the glow of the Law's immortal presence.

Such an organization would champion new styles of being economic, a word that originally meant "household management," instead of following corporate practices that are so obviously hurtful to the soul of the world. Such an organization would not rely upon criteria taken from elsewhere, but would develop standards and methods of valuation based on the defining metaphors of the Law itself. Corner offices would be for cornerstone people, and this judgment would not be debased by grounding it only in terms of money. Perhaps it would be someone who has given a lifetime of service, or a moral leader whose steadying and supporting strength belongs in a place of respect.

Sound crazy? If so, that is just a sign of how far we have fallen. But my view is that the Law shouldn't sit around and wait for things to become completely untenable. The crush of manic free market capitalism, which in the current environment is better called predatory capitalism, must be addressed with all the power and intelligence the Law can muster. What I wish for is an oasis of peace in the midst of all this economic blood-letting. I wish for a voice to cut through the haze of fear to speak with nobility, compassion, and devotion for another way of managing a household that doesn't make the members of the household feel they could be homeless at any moment. I want desperately to hear the beautiful and stabilizing voice of the Law. But where is it to be found?

A Special Talent

ONE OF THE great opportunities that work offers the imagination is the chance to interweave our efforts with those of others. I have worked in many different jobs over the years, and every now and then I have run across a person whose great talent was the ability to anticipate where the team was going, and then, in his or her own way, to facilitate that movement. Their work had a self-effacing quality, less concerned with making personal statements than with assisting the overall effort. To call such people "team players" doesn't quite get at what I'm alluding to. It was more particular, as if they knew *exactly* how to enter the imaginations both of their co-workers and the job itself. Their gift was choreographic; they knew just how and when to move things.

This special talent suffers when we embrace ideas that are antithetical to it. I hear from many people who work within organizations that encourage distance and fighting among their own members, insisting that each person compete with everyone else. In such an atmosphere, the real job becomes trying to bend others to my will so that when something gets done it will be clear who gets the credit. This in turn encourages strategies of manipulation and lethargy, so that when the phone rings with a call to service, my response is predicated not on a mutual desire to accomplish something, but on who's calling. If it's someone who can help or harm my personal situation, then I am helpful (read: ingratiating); if someone of "my level" or lower, then I am begrudging, and any work I actually "have" to do is likely half-assed because it doesn't directly benefit me.

We encourage such behavior by overly emphasizing the importance of individual achievement. Today's career strategies, for all their supposed sophistication, are adolescent at their core, calling out "Look at me, look at me!" But the talent I am referring to relies on being able to look outward, both to the project at hand and to the needs and talents of one's co-workers.

Another faulty idea that erodes the special talent of working together is job-based aristocracy. I know lawyers who think they are actually better than people in the mail room. As evidence for this, they point to their higher position (a phrase which of course begs the question), and the fact that they have more money, more education, and more toys. Like the early Calvinists who hoped against reason that worldly success might indicate future salvation, these lawyers try to deduce value from a mere job classification. But "lawyer" isn't better than "mail room clerk," only different. When people forget this, they forget that value doesn't belong with what we do, but with how we do what we do. Beauty and integrity lie in doing a good job, not in having one, and grace refers to style, not title.

A good example of what I'm talking about is a well-run kitchen in a busy restaurant. Half a dozen people in a space the size of a small office, working precisely in sync with each other, the nonstop orders, the food, and the wait staff. And all of this in the heat of the kitchen, with hot oil and sharp knives ready at hand. Talk about a pressure cooker! And yet the group moves in and out of the preparation, cooking, presentation, and cleaning up with efficiency, skill, and aesthetic pleasure. Who peels, who cooks, who garnishes, who serves, who eats

—all come together, each contribution necessary to the larger reality of a meal well served.

To be able to adapt one's natural styles to those of others in the name of a larger task—surely there is magic in this. I have worked with people who seemed to know not only what I wanted, but when and how. Things appeared before I even knew I needed them. Imagine how comforting it was for me to know not only that others were looking out for things, but that I actually existed in the mind of a supporting co-worker. And they did this not so I would be pleased with them, but simply because it was pleasing. When I was lucky enough to work with such a person, I found that soon I, too, was thinking this way, trying to imagine how I might shape my work to anticipate the needs of others on the team. Such an attitude seems wonderfully contagious. Except, of course, for the vaccine of self-interest, which stops the happy epidemic in its tracks.

When I was a young associate, a partner pulled me into his office for a bit of advice. He said I wasn't being aggressive enough within the firm, and that I wasn't being vocal enough in telling the partners that I worked for about my particular contributions and how important they were. He said I needed to be more forceful about showcasing my talents. Otherwise, he implied, I was going to get passed by.

This partner meant me well. He was trying to help me, and I appreciated it then and I appreciate it still. But the world he described is not one in which I will live. I will not beat my chest in front of folks who are supposed to be my colleagues. And I prefer to believe that if the members of a team have to lobby their leader to recognize their contributions, then the team has a bad leader. But most of all, I will not compete against peers with whom I share a mutual goal.

As for being passed by, I am content here in the kitchen. I enjoy peeling hard ideas to get at the tender sweetness within. I enjoy the long, slow simmering of the imagination, how it concentrates and intensifies flavor and color. I enjoy the heat and the smells, the bumping and jostling with my fellow workers on the line. And I enjoy watching how the many chefs that I work for take up, extend, and embellish my preparations. I am a simple ingredient, I like to imagine, useful in many recipes.

The Judge's Lot

THE VIEW that renders all suffering symptomatic and open to cure is thoroughly modern and thoroughly mistaken. It is as if we believe we are never supposed to endure pain, or feel depressed, or suffer despair, and that given enough drugs and therapy we can sail through a life of calm waters. And so we diagnose and drug anxious children instead of addressing the anxious world we adults have created for them, we drug our depression instead of rebelling against the manic cult of productivity, and we seek ways to cope with oppressions that our own apathy and fear allow to persist, all in the name of consistency and normalcy. We seem to have forgotten that consistency and normalcy *are not real states,* but are abstractions designed for use by a static mind.

Much of life goes against the grain of our personal wishes. Take, for example, the judge's lot. Lawyers might feel relative isolation in connection with their work, but judges suffer an exceptional isolation. Far more than the average lawyer, a judge must live within a very small cocoon.

At least lawyers still have other lawyers to talk to. But judges are forced by dint of their position to withdraw from the very legal culture in which they excelled. Many of the talents that led others to see them as worthy of a judgeship are the very talents that the judge is no longer allowed to use. Lunches with fellow lawyers become fewer, outings with old friends curtailed, long-standing associations bid farewell, and natural gregariousness restrained—all to honor the unattainable ideal of impartial Justice. So intense is this effort that judges must not only strive to *do* right but must bend over backwards to *appear* right. We call it avoiding the appearance of impropriety, but to the judge it must look like a very high hurdle indeed.

Why do judges have to avoid the appearance of impropriety? God knows if I had to live by that standard I'd never leave the house. But there is a great mystery in this simple rule, a rule that dominates the judge's life. The rule doesn't even make sense given our usual American belief that integrity and identity are self-contained. If I know in my heart that what I do is right and true, should it matter how it looks to others? But it does matter, largely because it takes the determination of what is right and true beyond the narcissistic grip of American individualism. Moreover, the rule emphasizes that a judge is not entirely human but also travels in a world in which image and appearance are as substantial as intent and action.

To suffer one's actions under popular scrutiny is a form of hopeless devotion. The judge represents Justice in this world, and if he or she is craven or crass, it calls into question our respect for Justice itself. Even if we sophisticate this rather unfair view and encourage the populace to be more tolerant of the judge's humanity, a subtle and impossible pressure remains on the judge to honor Justice by example.

Every judge lives within a shrunken world of human contact. The question is what can be done about it? Of course the judge can work to keep as many contacts with the outside world as possible. But it remains true that our jurisprudence requires judges to live isolated lives. We don't want our judges to be too involved with the people they must supervise, and avoiding the appearance of impropriety is meant to be a heavy restriction. Given this actual state of affairs, it is hardly symptomatic for judges to feel these restrictions. Instead of thinking only in terms of correction and cure, then, we might be more imaginative in finding ways for judges to live with their isolation.

What is a judge to do? One thing is to honor the fact that being a judge is hard, and that it sometimes hurts. Once we can engage the things that hurt us without moralism or attempts at cure, we have a much better chance of appreciating the values embedded in our pain. For example, the melancholy that we so often see in a judge's eyes is a gift of the pain of judging, and this melancholy is a necessary aspect of the judge's heavy task. In earlier times, the melancholy that judges often feel was associated with lead, a grey and dense metal considered necessary for deliberative concentration. Melancholy was a natural result of withdrawing from active life, and was associated with tasks that required such withdrawal, including artistic and scholarly pursuits. Unlike our knee-jerk manic response that would eradicate melancholy in the name of growth and progress, our forebears recognized that melancholy contains a kind of genius that must be respected. Slowness, stillness, and a sense of gravity —all essential to judging—are among the many moves and moods that melancholy allows. In Renaissance thought, melancholy was considered necessary for careful and dispassionate reflection.

I am not espousing some perverse "what doesn't kill you makes you stronger" machismo, and I certainly am not suggesting that judges should learn how to "cope" with their situations. I find few words uglier or more debilitating to the human spirit than coping. Coping originates from a victim mentality, a view of ourselves perpetuated by psychology itself. But coping is a pale substitute for what I am talking about. It is not coping to recognize that you cannot have life's pleasures and pains, one without the other. We are not victims, and we are not sick, simply because life can be hard.

I am encouraging a view that assumes life knows what it is doing. This is in keeping with a very old psychological maxim that whatever is there is necessary and whatever is necessary is there. If judges feel isolated because they *are* isolated, then such feelings are not symptomatic of anything wrong with the judge. Why not ask what values are hidden in these admittedly unpleasant feelings? I offer four possibilities and ask you to imagine more.

First, isolation concentrates intensity. As peripheral contacts shrink, those at the center become more focused, and this focus can be a source of great beauty, the world revealed in a rose. Very often, isolation leads judges to become more connected to their families than they were when they were practicing law. Could Justice be trying to tell us something here? Perhaps being a judge requires more intimacy with concerns of home and hearth than with the issues that often preoccupy lawyers. In Greek myth, Hestia, goddess of the hearth, was the central, enlivening point in both the city and the home and was considered essential for both. Judges need to be close to Hestia because they need the kind of focus ("hearth" comes from the Latin word for focus) she provides. She also was the first and last god to be honored in celebrations, which suggest that judges need her convivial gifts as much as they need her counterpart, Hermes, who was the god of communication and interpretation. Hence, the judge's isolation can be read as an attempt to intensify his or her connection with powers that were neglected during legal practice.

Second, if judges publicly acknowledged their isolation more they might teach the rest of us about the need for isolation in our own pursuits of justice. When tempers flare, or personal ambition inflames the soul, isolation often is needed to tame the flames. Judges can teach us this. It is a wonderful thing to watch a powerful person live with restraint, just as it is disgusting to watch power abused by selfish hands. Furthermore, if judges were more open about the difficulties of their calling they might become less reticent in reaching out to one another with compassion and understanding, the way cloistered groups have always reached out to one another for the strength and love required by their difficult callings.

Third, isolation suggests that the things the judge must give up are not necessary to the pursuit of justice. The fast-paced, aggressive, market-driven world of the practicing lawyer does not belong in the mind of the judge, despite efforts to reduce justice, along with everything else, to cost-benefit analyses. Instead, the judge must counter these simplistic extremes with circumspection, kindness, and values derived from places other than the bottom line. Similarly, under the old homeopathic principle of "like treats like," the more familiar the judge is with isolation the more he or she can call upon its perspectives when the judge needs to isolate something, such as a deep principle hidden among shallow arguments.

Lastly, the judge's isolation suggests that the judge does not live in a purely human world. Perhaps the judge must withdraw from human contact because the judge must become more familiar with contacts of another kind. Yes, the judge is lonely; but is he or she truly alone? The principle of retreat resonates throughout spiritual traditions (to which judgeship belongs), whether it be monks retiring to a monastery, religious mystics going into the desert or up the mountain, or Native American and aboriginal traditions of vision quests and walkabouts. Retreat is essential for spiritual traditions; it adds weight to the ephemeral and coalesces the spirit's natural dispersion. Retreat is valuable not because it leaves the spiritual initiate alone, but because it connects the initiate with the invisible powers of spiritual life. Especially in a materialistic world hell-bent on eradicating soul and spirit, the judge's isolation can be seen as a godsend, a small island in the midst of a troubled sea (the Latin root of "isolation" means "island").

So I ask your indulgence for what ails you. For the judge, as for the rest of us, the task is to hear and heed the *logos* of the *psyche,* the telling of the soul. It may be true that no person is an island, but that does not mean there are no islands, or that we are not sometimes called to their isolated shores.

Living on Legal Time

THERE ARE MANY different kinds of time. There are six time zones in the United States alone, and God knows how many around the world. And clock time is only one kind of time. Everyday language recognizes different kinds of time happening in different places, such as doing something in a New York second, or settling into island time. Danny Flowers wrote a song about living on Tulsa time, and Jimmy Buffett croons about "living and dying in three-quarters time."

We all experience the qualitative diversity of time. Compare twenty minutes spent waiting to hear what the doctor has to say about your tests with that spent reading or watching television or making love or waiting for the water to boil. "Twenty minutes" might suggest that the same amount of time has passed in each event, but they are not equal in terms of temporal experience.

A carpenter working on the soft curve of a hand-finished chair leg works in a different time than does a floor trader for the stock exchange. Neither kind of time is more real than the other, nor is one better or worse. But they are different. Lived time, in distinction to clock and calendar time, is a function of many influences. Place seems to matter, as does the nature of the task at hand. The chair leg tells the carpenter how fast to go, while the tropical sun melts away hardened attitudes of how long things are supposed to take.

All goes well in this temporal quilt as long as we remember that every purpose under heaven has its time. But things begin to fray if we try to collapse one kind of time into another. The New Yorker in St. Somewhere can yell and throw things while the airplane mechanic takes a nap under the now-two-hours-late-taking-off plane, but to no avail. You can't turn back time, and you can't turn it ahead, either. You can't change time simply by resetting your watch, and you can't rush things just because you are in a rush.

This message is timely for lawyers because the legal profession increasingly is losing touch with its own kind of time. Instead of relying on the kind of time that comes with the legal imagination, legal practice is too quick to emulate the speedy world of entrepreneurial business. More and more, better legal service has come to mean quicker legal service.

Surveys suggest that lawyers are working longer hours now than ever before. The usual explanation given for this increase is the same as we hear in other sectors of public life —there is more work to be done by fewer people as a result of competition. Perhaps. But if you look at this increase from the point of view of numerous kinds of time, you might wonder if lawyers are working longer because you can only speed up the work lawyers do to a certain point and, after that, if you want to do more you're simply going to have to work longer. In other words, what is out of kilter are two different temporal worlds.

Law is meant to be slower than the overall pace of society, to lag behind a bit. Lawyers therefore must be willing to be sticks in the mud, dragging their feet and waiting to see what happens. Lawyers are highly trained to analyze precisely, consider carefully, and act appropriately. The lawyer therefore works in a kind of time similar to that of the academic or the artist, which is perhaps why when lawyers leave legal practice they so often go into such fields. It is as if they are searching for a more natural temporal home than is being offered by the pace of practice.

The fast-lane folks don't like the fact that law takes the time it does. They get fidgety when lawyers won't give them a quick answer so they can get on with the deal making. That's too bad, but it is essential. If law is to perform its regulating function, then it must resist efforts to let the horses of ambition run away with us. It strikes me that legal time is one of the law's greatest gifts, and that a lawyer who allows a client or a situation to unduly rush the law and its work does a disservice to all.

Nothing enrages a mind in a hurry more than feeling stalled or frustrated, as every lawyer knows who has ever had to counsel a client to put on the brakes. Clients sometimes call lawyers naysayers and outsiders, accuse them of not being team players, and even threaten that, if the lawyer can't get things done in a timely fashion (i.e., the *client's* time), then business will be taken elsewhere. Countering such demands is extraordinarily difficult, but luckily the kind of careful judgment required for countering them is precisely the kind of judgment that arises from legal time. It's a mystery all right, but then what isn't?

Lawyers need to remember, and to remind others, that every job requires its own kind of time to be done well. This probably never will be easy or welcomed, but then the law is intended to be a bit anachronistic. Maybe we need a song to encourage us. Ready? One, two, three, four, "Living on legal time . . ."

The Good, the Bad, and the Ugly

I WANT TO RECOUNT some of the lawyers I have known who should not be lawyers. Not many, but too many. One said that everyone living in what he called "Third World" countries should be sterilized because they don't measure up to his white-bread view of civilization. Others have hated either men or women, depending on which manner of chauvinism they specialized in. Some have hated people who were gay, while others have hated people who weren't. In fact, I've known lawyers who have pretty much covered the waterfront of bigotry, hating anyone not like themselves for that reason alone. And of course there are those who think that being poor is a sure sign of either laziness or inferiority.

I've known lawyers who have lied to cover their own mistakes, and others who have used the sheer size of their firms to intimidate and bully. I've known lawyers who have rejoiced at "winning" motions and cases that they knew they shouldn't have won. And I've known lawyers, and know of one former judge very much in the news, who have abused the power invested in them for ideological and political motives.

The sad fact is that many of these lawyers are considered to be successful. Many sit in big offices in big firms, drawing big salaries and acting for all the world like big shots. Many of them win a lot of cases. And many of them project carefully constructed facades of integrity. But, in my view, winning cases, accumulating wealth, and holding power does not make a lawyer a good lawyer, only a rich, winning, powerful lawyer.

If such lawyers are at the extreme end of a spectrum, there are others who fall short of such outrageous views and conduct but who nonetheless tarnish the practice of law. Unfortunately, I've known too many lawyers who are simply rude and ill-mannered. To use a minor example, I can think of more than once that I've given a speech to a group of lawyers only to have one or two sitting there reading a newspaper, or going through files, or chatting with each other, oblivious to their rudeness. They would say, of course, that they can do more than one thing at a time, and that is true. But what you can do and what you should do are not always the same thing, or at least that's what I was taught when I was growing up.

I know that such remarks are moralistic, and as a psychologist moral claims are not properly part of my discipline. But I am speaking here as a lawyer, and I think it is the duty of every lawyer to raise moral issues when necessary, and to proclaim the bad seeds of our profession for what they are.

Let me be clear. I think lawyers are supposed to be noble, honorable, trustworthy, and loyal. I think no person should hear words of bigotry or hatred issue from a lawyer's lips. I think no lawyer should ever use power to harm, intimidate, or belittle. Lawyers should not be chauvinists, racists,—phobes of any kind, ideologues, or people of meager character. They should not display bad manners. They should be courteous, peaceful if at all possible, and, above all, they should use the mantle of their office and the power of their learning to protect and serve the weak, the indigent, and the oppressed.

When I was growing up, lawyers were figures of great respect, both in the sense that people respected them and that they showed great respect themselves. People knew they could be trusted to keep secrets and to help those in need. They did not go for ostentatious displays of wealth because such displays seemed inappropriate for servants, which is how those lawyers tended to think of themselves. What has happened, I wonder.

Allow me this request and claim. If you see yourself as one of the bad seeds that I have identified, either learn to free yourself from your small-mindedness or please quit being a lawyer. I ask this because bad lawyers are more than bad lawyers, they are anti-lawyers, and their cheap views and conduct harm the valuable work of the many, many good and decent lawyers who struggle each day to do right by a profession that many cultures say lies at the heart of what it means to be civilized. If you are a bad lawyer, and if anywhere in what remains of your soul there is the least bit of affection or respect for the law, please leave. It is the least you can do to make right what you have undone.

And, for the vast majority of lawyers (I pray) who are not bad lawyers, I ask you to raise up your voices to proclaim the nudity of these false emperors. It is our duty to police our own, and this duty goes beyond turning in lawyers who break the letter of the law. They are the easy ones to identify and expel. Far worse are the ones who don't break the letter of the law but abuse its spirit. They are the ones who have broken their vows; they are the ones who cause the law to weep. They are not to be trusted, admired, or encouraged, but deserve to be drummed out of a beautiful practice they can only make ugly.

So to every lawyer I say—beware transient social standards of success. Please remember that our profession lies outside of time, belonging to the immortal play of Justice. Turn instead to the sacred vows that each of us took, and measure every lawyer accordingly. None of us is pure, and none of us can always do the right thing, but our fellow citizens must know that we are doing our best.

PART THREE

A World in Need of Attention

IN CLASSICAL and Renaissance thought, the world was enlivened by soul. This is in stark contrast to our modern view that soul is a possession of the individual person, and that the greater world of animals, plants, and things is mere soulless matter acting in accord with immutable instinct and physical law. How extraordinarily mistaken we are in such beliefs, as if the joy in a dog's eye or the affectionate embrace of an old and well-worn sweater is of our making, projections from our subjectivity onto the blank screen of a world that would not exist but for us.

The extent and ramifications of this mistake cannot be overstated. It leads to feelings of isolation, offers false justifications for environmental abuse, and insults our fellow inhabitants of our world. Psychology, too, that discipline named for soul, has contributed to this great mistake with its dualistic theories about objective and subjective reality, its therapeutic models that assume all suffering emanates from some secret, private Self that is not properly part of the world, and its general neglect and ignorance of the ongoing life of the soul in all the facets of worldly life.

The essays in this section contribute to the old idea of the "anima mundi," or ensouled world, urging us to be more open-minded in our conceptions of soul and its place and more willing to attend to the needs of soul wherever they appear. So much of what feels personal to us, so much of what people bring to therapy, are actually examples of a world in need of proper attention and care.

A short anecdote can help make the point. A woman once grew angry with me in therapy and declared, "You care more about this building than you do about me." She was wrong that I cared more about the building, but not wrong that I cared as much about the building, which, like people, can also be anorectic or depressed and in need of care. To my mind, the job of therapy is to attend to soul, not the whinings of the Self with its nagging insistence that it must come first and be all that matters. A psychology unable to care for the soul of buildings, or to learn about soul from the many things of the world, is a psychology unworthy of the name, and so the essays in this section attempt to move psychology out of the consulting room and into the street, urging that psychological care often requires political action dedicated to the soul of the world.

The Dangers of Deadspeak

THERE ISN'T ANYTHING necessarily wrong with jargon. Sure, we have a right to get mad when someone uses jargon as a smokescreen or to imply that we aren't "in the know," but that's a sign of rudeness or incompetence on the part of the speaker, not something innately bad about jargon itself.

So this isn't an attack on jargon as such. What I am concerned about is a style of jargon that has crept into the everyday language of business and law. Linguists probably have a name for what I'm talking about, but I don't know what to call it. I recognize it mostly by how it feels, or, more precisely, I recognize it by its *calculated absence of feeling.*

Not so long ago, if you lost your job you "got fired" or maybe "laid off." Recently, these terms have been replaced with a succession of new ones. "Reduction in force" (sometimes itself reduced to "RIF") was the phrase of choice for a while, and then came "downsizing" and "rightsizing." Just the other day I heard a new one: "decruited."

Notice how the farther along this list you go, the further you get from the reality behind the words—people losing their livelihoods. Each successive term is designed to sound more objective than its predecessors, although it's hard to miss the self-satisfied smugness of "rightsizing." These words aren't meant to communicate specialized knowledge among specialists, which is what jargon does when it is used properly, but rather to convey real-life experiences in a manner that sterilizes them of their emotional, societal, and moral dimensions. Such language reminds me of the time I heard a munitions expert talk about "soft targets." It took me a minute to catch his meaning, but when did I know one soft target who got goose bumps.

Let's make up our own word for this kind of language. Let's call it "deadspeak." After all, the intention of a word like "decruited" is to kill the reality behind the word, and to imply that we are talking about objective processes—you know, "decruit" is simply the opposite of "recruit." Nobody's losing a job here, we're just "restructuring" and "re-engineering" the corporate machine to extract the highest productivity for the least possible cost. The core metaphors from which deadspeak derives are coldly mechanical and economic, not human.

Deadspeak anesthetizes us to the actuality of our actions. Moreover, deadspeak itself seems blissfully detached from reality. So what if less than half of all companies "downsized" since 1988 have improved profits, or that barely one-third have increased their productivity? No matter. Deadspeak manages by slogan and doesn't depend on actual results. It pulls off this charade by insisting on defining the very terms by which it is to be judged, terms and definitions that are fluid to say the least. If projections aren't met, then deadspeak says to "cut more overhead" (fire more people) or "stimulate productivity" (crack the whip). But never, never question the efficacy or ethics of the projections themselves, or of those who create them.

We know that many workers have lost respect for their employers. Worse, many have lost faith in loyalty itself. Talk to someone who has survived a "downsizing," and, if they aren't too afraid to talk, they will tell you about crushed expectations and ugly cover-your-ass cynicism. Who can blame remaining workers for being suspicious and guarded? After all, they know that they are being evaluated by people who, at best, think of them as "assets" or "profit centers"—as if such terms are compliments worthy of human beings. In an environment that is hostile to the idea that humans have intrinsic worth apart from their potential to generate capital, we should not be surprised to find selfish and dispirited workers. We are fast becoming a nation of individual contractors in an age of broken promises.

No wonder workers increasingly are unwilling to go out of their way unless there's "something in it for them." The blindspot is not seeing that it is the deadspeak mentality that is driving workers into their self-contained exiles. Just where else do we think workers learn this kind of protectionist and paranoid thinking? In church?

Do you remember when workers used to be called "personnel"? I'll grant you that "personnel" isn't a particularly graceful word, but at least it has "person" in it. Deadspeak prefers "human resources," and talks about "human resource management" as a means of "maximizing productivity." In the mind of deadspeak, humans are like deposits of coal or stands of timber—fuel for the engine of productivity.

Things have gotten downright comical. One company decided its workers needed to be "empowered." The inevitable expert was hired. Then came a memorandum requiring workers to attend a *mandatory* meeting on empowerment. To quote Dave Barry, I swear I'm not making this up.

Comical, yes, but treacherous. I grew up in the South during the civil rights movement, and I remember a friend telling me at the time that white people couldn't "give" black people freedom and equality, that all white people could do was to take them away. Now, years later, when I hear "empowerment," I cannot help but hear a backhanded insult perpetrated by oppressors to belittle and control the oppressed. Good intentions cannot overcome the fact that deadspeak, by its very nature, works against human integrity.

It is difficult to place deadspeak's discriminatory arrogance with precision because it goes to such lengths to sound neutral and correct. This blandness makes it easy for people to use deadspeak without realizing what they're doing. Usually, listening to someone use jargon unconsciously is at worst irritating. But deadspeak is dangerous. It gives voice to a style of imagining that erodes our communal faith in loyalty and weakens our innate capacities for compassion and sympathetic understanding. If deadspeak destroys these things, then the atrocities have just begun.

What It Means to Be Lean and Mean

I CAN'T HELP IT. To me, some of the images held up to us as desirable are offensive. I have written about the ugliness of words like "rightsizing" and "decruiting," and have complained about the ability of such words to anesthetize us to the reality behind them. I have called such words "deadspeak," and have warned of the insidious trend in our culture toward a language that lacks sensuality and attachment, thereby mirroring our modern malaise of isolation and loneliness.

But not all of our catch phrases are so lifeless. One, in particular, seems to point to the return of a kind of repressed anger or hostility that is in stark contrast to the blandness of words like "human resources." Curiously, it usually is found in the company of deadspeak, and of other words like "competition" and "global economy."

"Lean and mean." That's what we're supposed to be. It applies to everything, from the individual to the company to the country. We're all supposed to be lean and mean.

When we say that we want to be lean and mean, I think we mean that we want to be energetic, to get rid of all extraneous drains on our time and energy, and to be alert for opportunities. We want to be efficient, and not bogged down in unnecessary procedures or regulations. We want the lowest overhead and the highest productivity. We want to be tough and resilient.

O.K. Fine. Let's say for the sake of argument that such things are desirable. But we do a disservice to the image of "lean and mean" if we stop there. The important thing to remember about adopting an image like "lean and mean" is that when we adopt an image we adopt it in its entirety. We can't just take some aspects of the image and leave the rest behind. And the more we focus only on one part or another of an image, the more likely we are to play out the others unconsciously.

So what else do we become when we become "lean and mean?" What does this image really mean, exactly and completely?" Best I can tell, it means to get rid of the fat, to trim the bulging waistline of middle management, to train aerobically fit employees who have the stamina to keep at it, never slowing down or stopping, always working out, always searching for new opportunities. To be lean and mean is to be aggressive, predatory, hungry, and fit for the fight. Lean and mean moves fast, isn't tied down by relationships or commitments, works better alone, is quick on its feet, and has reflexes honed for attack. Lean and mean can be ruthless, going for the jugular, winning at all costs. And it can be paranoid, frightened, and dangerous. Taken together, it sounds like a junkyard dog to me.

There is much ugliness in the phrase "lean and mean." Think how, in our hunger for a fatless *corpus* (body), individuals, corporations, and the body politic have all become trapped in a kind of anorectic economics—wanting sustenance without substance, no longer valuing the things of an agricultural or manufacturing economy but instead trying to live on ethereal ideas of information. Think about the constant dieting, working out, staying in shape, roaming, and restlessness occasioned by a life lived "lean and mean."

Think about how bad-tempered we are becoming.

In a perverse way, the "lean and mean" approach has actually delivered on its economic promises by creating a marketplace of sparse returns and dispirited workers. Having "cut to the bone," we have suddenly found ourselves unattractive, without curve or contour. In its efforts to eliminate all but the barest of support, "lean and mean" has created a workforce of well-muscled skeleton crews competing overtime in a dog-eat-dog world.

I know I'm laying it on thick, but we really need to snap out of it. The clichés and catch-phrases that we adopt more or less unconsciously aren't just idle playthings. They affect our souls. Once they take root in our imaginations, they grow of their own accord and reach into every corner of our psychological life. We can make efforts to trim them back and to keep them contained, but they continue to grow back, sometimes threatening to choke off other, perhaps long-standing, beliefs and ideals.

The answer, it seems to me, is to pay more attention to what kind of seed we plant in our imaginations. Is "lean and mean" *really* an image you want growing in your soul? Maybe so. If so, then set your expectations accordingly. For that matter, maybe the question is moot, seeing as how the "lean and mean" image already is so widely dispersed. I'm reminded of the fast-growing kudzu vine in the South and the zebra mussel that now is spreading through our waterways. Maybe "lean and mean" is like that, a troublesome thing that's nonetheless here to stay. Maybe all we can do now is to be aware of it and try to keep it under control.

Still, I think we should consider some alternatives to "lean and mean." It strikes me as altogether too limited an image to sustain the life of an individual, a company, or a country. I don't have any ready-made clichés to replace it, but surely we can come up with something more beautiful, something more . . . well, noble. Who knows, even a small step such as the one we have taken here from talking in savage, animal terms to talking about tending plants and cultivating our imaginations might help. Farmers and gardeners, you know, have fertile imaginations. But if we're going to keep that junkyard dog around, can somebody at least feed him? He's making me nervous.

Fears Ignite When Tragedy Strikes Close

On Thursday, July 1, 1993, a gunman walked into the law offices of Pettit & Martin in San Francisco with a briefcase full of semiautomatic weapons. When the shooting was over, he had killed eight people and wounded six others before killing himself. The following appeared July 6, 1993, in the *San Francisco Daily Journal.*

WE WILL never know why.

As the police investigation of last Thursday's tragedy at Pettit & Martin unfolds, we can expect to hear numerous theories about what motivated the gunman to do what he did. The cryptic letter found on his body will be combed for hidden meanings, as will the list of television programs and other notes found in his briefcase. Already the news accounts are starting to contain more details about the gunman's past as the media, like the rest of us, struggle to find a clue, any clue, as to why.

But we will never know why.

Perhaps it is just this that tightens the knot in our stomachs. We know there are shootings every day, but they happen down there, on the streets, not here, thirty floors up. A back alley, a gangway, a darkened corner—that is where the violence is. Not here, not in a conference room, not in my office.

It all just seems so out of place, the terror deepened by its sheer incongruity. Despite, or maybe because of, our daily diet of violence we somehow manage to convince ourselves that we, at least, are safe. Above it all. And then Thursday happens and we feel the fear, the same fear that they feel on the street, the same fear that peers into the darkened windows of each passing car, watching for the fiery spit of indiscriminate death.

The murders at Pettit & Martin are neither more nor less horrible because of where they occurred or to whom. This time it happened to be a law firm instead of the World Trade Center, or a post office, or a Texas cafeteria. And yet there is no denying that when tragedy strikes so close to home it ignites our fears in ways that these more distant events cannot. We begin to think. "Why I was over there just this morning." Or, "I had an appointment there this afternoon." Or, "My God, I was probably in the building when he was."

Television can bring us images of coughing and sooted workers streaming from the World Trade Center, or show us the hopeless eyes of a refugee, but still there is a remoteness to these images that helps us to remain aloof, detached, protected. But this is not so remote. We know that building; we have been on those elevators. Perhaps we know people who knew those whom we have lost. Perhaps they were our friends, our loved ones. But at the very least we all share the sickening reality that it could have been our friends. It could have been us.

As a psychotherapist I guess I should have some answers. I should be able to tell you how to handle the horror, how to make sense out of it, how to fit it into your life in a way that will cause the least disruption. But I can't. And even if I could, I wouldn't. I wouldn't because then the violence would lose its horror and as a people we can no longer afford the luxury of settled contentment.

I wouldn't because I refuse to turn Thursday's tragedy into an excuse for introverted self-examination. I know that as lawyers we are accustomed to a certain level of societal abuse, but it seems that the stakes are rising. Beer commercials glibly depict lawyers as rodeo cattle to be roped and tied, and blockbuster movies feature lawyers either being eaten by dinosaurs or as greedy murderers who deserve what they get.

And now this.

But we must be more compassionate than our detractors. Thursday's atrocity is especially painful because it has touched us so directly, but our fear is pointing outward too, into the street and now into the high-rise havens that we thought could protect us. Our fear is trying to help us by showing us where the problems really are: out there, where a man bent on killing can legally buy an arsenal fit for combat and enough ammunition to do far worse than he did.

That is what our fear is trying to say, that we have *reason* to be afraid, that there really *is* danger in the world, and that the answer doesn't lie in "coping" or in beefing up our security but in crafting active responses to a world in need of care.

There are other feelings, too, feelings other than fear.

We have lost friends and colleagues and so it is time for mourning. I have heard soldiers talk of an almost mystical tie that connects them with their fallen comrades. Police officers have a similar bond I think, as do others whose job or station in life puts them in harm's way. As a profession we, too, must feel the communal sting of what has happened. It is so tempting to pass the grief by writing off the entire incident as one more crazy gunman run amok. But the repressed will return and so this is no answer.

A better way is to acknowledge that in our mutual grief lies the greatest measure of our humanity. Through it we honor the dead while we begin to rebuild our communal courage.

Talk to one another. Share your tears. Light a candle. Say

a prayer. However you decide to do it, the important thing is to observe the loss and to remember. Our colleagues have fallen and they deserve no less.

But don't let it stop there. The next time you read about a child killed by a stray bullet, remember how you feel now. Remember how it feels to have blind terror strike so close to home. It seems to me that the greatest respect we can show for those who die so innocently and unexpectedly is to reaffirm our insoluble bonds with them. On a dirty stoop or in a polished office, violence and death taste the same. Even the highest skyscraper is forever cemented in the streets below.

We feel helpless now—but there are things we can do. We can give grief the time it needs. We can reaffirm our communal bond. We can let our fear show us the enemy. We can sustain our outrage and we can act.

But we will never know why.

Destructive Listening

I WAS IN a book store the other day and picked up a book on communication. The book gave 20 rules for effective communication. "Listening" came in at number 19.

I'm surprised it made the list at all. Who listens anymore? For all of the talking we do, when's the last time you were actually listened to, actually heard?

One reason listening gets so little respect is that it is too passive for the American mind. The very posture and mood of listening, supine and receptive, goes against our active nature. The important thing to the American mind is that I get my say, that my voice be heard, that I be free to shout my views from the mountaintops. Even our most basic ideas of freedom of expression focus almost entirely on the right of people to actively voice their opinions and beliefs. But surely there also must be freedom to listen.

When I looked up Rule 19, I learned that the key to "good" listening is to be an "active listener." See what I mean? Even when we finally get around to listening, we find a way to interject action into it. Listening becomes something else to do, like managing our stress and maximizing our productivity. You see how all of this is in keeping with our one-sided cultural preference for activity. The active listener doesn't sit back and let the conversation wash over him or her. No, the active listener leans forward, attentively watches the person speaking, nods and interjects so as to reassure and encourage the speaker, and is alert for speaker's feelings. In short, an active listener listens like a golden retriever listens.

Another listening symptom I've noticed is destructive listening. This is a big one in the American mind. Right now, right this second, how are you listening to me? Chances are you are listening to see whether or not I am right, and whether you agree with what I am saying. You are listening for contradictions or inconsistencies in my "argument," *which is what this style of listening assumes my speech to be,* and you are trying to relate what I am saying to you and your life. This style of listening proceeds on the basis of analysis and assumes that the listener must react to what is being said in some way, usually through a showing of assent or rejection.

You can hear the problem as soon as I say it, right? This is a style of listening that prevents listening. My true sound cannot come through if it has to go through your personal filter first. To listen in terms of right or wrong or agreement or disagreement muffles my voice with moralistic overlays and narcissistic hubris. Moralistic because it erects a standard not derived from what the speaker is saying; narcissistic because all we want to hear are echoes of our own voices.

These prevailing styles of listening fuel our already desperate attempts to be heard. If I know everyone is listening to me in ways that subsume what I am saying, then of course I will turn up the volume, straining to be heard over the din of warring listeners. If only someone would actually listen to us, perhaps we wouldn't have to shout so.

How, then, to become more adept listeners? That is the question.

The psychologist James Hillman is fond of talking about the need simply to entertain ideas without immediately rushing to decide how to apply them. So many wonderful ideas die right there, in the premature rush to see whether they will "work" or not. But who cares whether they will work? Can't we allow ideas that dance and frolic in our minds for no reason other than they are enjoyable company? Can't we sit all night and talk of our unattainable dreams and ideals, drunk on the sound of one another's voices, safely held in one another's fantasies? Or have we become so obsessed and dogmatic in our manic drive for efficiency and economic productivity that we simply can't allow such detours?

We would do well to take seriously what Dr. Hillman is saying. Unless we learn to entertain ideas and make them feel welcome, they might decide to stop coming to visit. No one likes a host who makes you feel like you are intruding.

The word "listen" is derived from a root word for "ear." An old definition of "listen" was "to give ear to," and of course we have "Friends, Romans, countrymen, lend me your ears." To listen, then, is to make a contribution of one's hearing to the speaker, it is an act of devotion. In classical thought, hearing was the highest sense bestowed by Hermes, the great messenger god, bringer of dreams, and emissary between the world of the living and the underworld of the dead. This suggests that listening includes hearing the undertones and aspirations, the hidden implications and tricky twists of what is being said. For this kind of listening, developing the ear is paramount. To listen well means to have a trained, educated, and appreciative ear, like a musician who spends a lifetime listening so he or she might better hear the music.

Listening for something in particular can be very useful when trying to relate what is being said to certain ideas already held in mind. But the limitations of such styles of listening are similarly clear. Listening for something in particular is like listening with a checklist in hand. The list soon takes priority over what is being said, becoming a kind of voiceover. And of course we all know we rarely hear more than we listen for.

So allow me to say that listening is number one in my book. I ask for a renewed respect for listening and urge that we practice trying simply to hear one another. We can always argue, but can we lend our ears? Can we replace aggression and hyperactivity with appreciation and hospitality as guiding themes in our listening? Can we at least give such questions a hearing?

New Year's Resolutions

WELL, it's that time of the year again. It's time to make resolutions for the coming year. I used to think the entire notion of "years" was an abstraction. After all, there have been many calendars and ways of imagining time that are every bit as real for those who follow them as the modern notion of time is for us. Philosophers long ago pointed out the profound difference between the objective, measurable time of scientific thought and the subjective *experience* of time as duration itself. The former usually is imagined as a calculus of linear motion, while the latter is imagined in more qualitative terms. The former is predictable and uniform, the latter variable and uncertain—someone can be "wise beyond their years," we say, or "a kid at heart." And a twenty-minute thunderstorm will be different temporal experiences for the sailor at sea and the meteorologist ashore watching the same storm on a radar screen.

I guess now that I say it I still think all of that is true. But now I think something else is true, too. I think we are all born into an ongoing world beyond our final comprehension, and talking about "years" doesn't have to lock us into clock time but can help us imagine the cycles, enduring patterns, and unexpected occurrences that mark our passage. It is the reduction of "years" into a narrowly imagined mathematical construct that is the mistake. But when we allow "years" to denote a vibrant and variable experience, then the idea of "years" becomes a tender way of imagining that which passes. In fact, the etymology of "year" is "that which passes."

Anyway, my task here is to make resolutions for the coming year, so no more putting things off. I refuse, however, to go this alone. So I've made a list for all of us. Misery loves company.

Number One. I resolve to be more gentle in my dealings with my fellow citizens and with the world we all share. Anyone who has lived through the past ten years or so will, I hope, see the unquestioned need for this one.

Number Two. Lose ten pounds. It seems everyone I know wants to lose ten pounds, regardless of whether they're waifs or fifty pounds overweight. I hereby also give full liberty to take "ten pounds" metaphorically, and to measure it according to your own weighted criteria.

Number Three. I resolve not to be a sucker for every shyster who tries to justify incivility in the name of "increased competition." Let's be clear. When we justify our conduct by saying there is "increased competition," what we really are saying is that *we* are being increasingly competitive. "Competition" in a civilized environment is supposed to be a conscious activity carried on by thinking people, but words such as "competition," "free market," and " productivity" have increasingly become passive/aggressive talismans used to justify all kinds of bad behavior. Haven't you had enough? I mean, really. Aren't you sick and tired of the manic, anxious, and increasingly mean-spirited drills we've been putting ourselves through? Is the way you feel right now the way you want to feel? In your heart of hearts, do you think it's how you're supposed to feel? I resolve to remember that America's ideals cannot be limited to building a powerful economic engine. From the beginning, the main idea for America has been to craft a more perfect union honoring *all* inalienable rights. "America the Beautiful," the song says. So I resolve to remember that justice and beauty are just as important in measuring how we are doing as are economic standards of competition, productivity, and profit. Besides, competition isn't supposed to drive civilization but to contribute to civilization's grander goals. Civilized competition can be a wonderful thing, but not competition that succumbs to barbarism or aspires to tyranny. In fact, now that I think about it, my personal resolution is not to compete at all. I think I'll just take a year off and not compete. And while I'm at it, I resolve not to be ambitious, either. I feel ten pounds lighter already.

Number Four. I resolve to enjoy things more. I'm tired of feeling caught at an indeterminate point between past and future. This is the time problem again, and I resolve to pay more attention to the qualitative experience of that which passes. As the Jimmy Buffet song says, "Go fast enough to get there, but slow enough to see." That means spending more time on the sensual things of life. Good food, friends, late-night talks, the incredible fact of writing or whatever it is for you that carries your soul. I resolve to taste more acutely, smell more subtly, touch more lingeringly. I resolve to hear more music in the sounds of the world. And I resolve to see with a more discerning eye that which is shown to me.

Number Five. I resolve to educate my imagination as well as my mind. The modern mind has become too limited in its capacities for imagination, which in turn has weakened various talents such as creativity, inventiveness, compassion, and empathy. Most people nowadays educate only a small part of their imaginative potential, usually, again, because they spend so much time either competing or getting ready to compete. I don't know yet what I'm going to do, maybe learn a new language or listen to more music. But I resolve to imagine more.

So there you have it. Now that I've said all them, they

actually seem doable. I know from past experience, though, how hard it is to keep resolutions. But it'll be easier this time, knowing we're all going through the same thing. It'll help me be more patient just knowing that you'll be trying, too. And I especially like knowing I can count my ten pounds the way you're going to count yours.

Happy New Year.

A Note on Pragmatism

AMERICA has always been busy making things happen. For much of its life, America has been faced with tough circumstances, and rarely has it been able to relax its guard. America has kept its motor revved up because it has been cold outside, and still today it remains intent on finding more efficient ways to keep honed for a world declared hostile by modern thought. And if America retains much of its frontier practicality and no-nonsense attitude, could it be because until very recently it still *was* a frontier town? Although few major cities have been born in Europe since the sixteenth century, no American city existed before then. America may be the oldest continuing democracy, but it still is young by worldly standards.

We could think of this and many other good reasons why America prefers practicality. But there is an exuberance to America's practicality that transcends such reasoning. It's as if America simply loves to make things happen, and to invent and produce things to make them happen. America loves coming up with its own ideas and ways of doing things, even if it often makes the mistake of assuming newer necessarily means better. Is it mere accident that the same mind to declare independence also spawned numerous inventions and improvements, and received a gold medal from the Agricultural Society of Paris for inventing the moldboard plow?

The philosophy that best holds America's free-thinking

practicality is pragmatism. Although nominally a creation of the late nineteenth century, we might imagine the pragmatic spirit as endemic to the American experience—given with the territory. Pragmatism is an American product that many consider to be America's most influential contribution to formal philosophy, and it has turned out to be philosophy of the most powerful kind; it is lived more than thought. "Pragmatism," "practical," and "practice" all derive from a root word meaning "action." Pragmatism exists in the very musculature of America's habitual daily actions, and is in turn made self-evident by the very actions that rely on it.

As originally conceived by Charles Peirce (1839–1914), pragmatism insists that the meaning or truth of an idea depends not on an individual's conception of it as true (the Cartesian viewpoint), but on its publicly verifiable character. Pragmatism therefore turned attention away from individual consciousness as the sole arbiter of meaning and truth, and toward the world and society. It found ready allies in the tools of scientific experimentation and logical analysis with their demands for objective verification and consistency. Pragmatism spoke the same language as these other styles of thought, sharing a common rhetoric addressed to actions and reactions, observations and predictions, experimentation and demonstrable results.

From the very beginning, though, pragmatists disagreed over the nature and compass of pragmatism. For example, the role and extent of subjectivity in pragmatic judgment was hotly debated among leading pragmatists such as Peirce, William James, and John Dewey. But despite such disagreements, one theme remained central to their collectively pragmatic world-view: what matters most about an idea or a course of conduct are its *consequences* in the world of public action.

In everyday life, pragmatism appears overtly in demands that things be "practical." But what do we mean, exactly? In general, we probably mean pretty much what the early pragmatists meant—that the object of inquiry be judged according to its publicly verifiable consequences by the standards of experimental science and logical analysis. The practical question is "What are the consequences of this or that course of action?" But please note that pragmatism's reliance on pragmatic methods and definitions is self-referential. Pragmatism decides what is relevant according to its own standards, and then uses these results to defend the standards themselves. In other words, the main reason practical talk sounds more realistic than other ways of talking is *because pragmatism presents itself in realistic terms.* Proclaiming what is real and relevant is characteristic of pragmatism's rhetoric and mood.

We hear this rhetoric and mood in the early pragmatists. William James described practical consequences in terms of what "pays" or "works," and intended both terms to refer to a thing or idea's usefulness for *human* purposes. For John Dewey, being practical meant "the rule of referring all thinking, all reflective considerations, to consequences for final meaning and test." Practically speaking, said Dewey, "[t]hat which satisfactorily terminates inquiry is, by definition, knowledge."

Such phrases give us a better picture of America's pragmatism. We see it is humanistic in intent and obsessive by character. Humanistic because it relies on human satisfaction as its prime value; obsessive because it seeks to gather *all* thinking under its rubric. We also see that pragmatism has delusions about stopping inquiry and establishing "final meaning" and "knowledge." And even in its earliest formulations pragmatism already reveals affiliations with another dominant complex in the American mind—bottom line economics. James could have been a modern-day CEO when he declared an idea's meaning or truth to be a function of its "cash value."

The question that has always plagued pragmatism, though, is how to justify limiting relevant consequences in this manner. When pragmatism speaks of "consequences" does it mean only those things that are experimentally verifiable (Peirce), or does it include efficacious beliefs such as religious faiths (James), or does it mean only assertions warranted by logical inquiry and justification (Dewey)? And what about the many aspects of experience that simply are not demonstrable in some objective, repeatable way?

Such questions have never been settled by those who devote their lives to such pursuits. But everyday America seems to have simply decided that "practical" means "measurably better according to some objective standard." Very often, the next step is to translate this quest for practical measurement into economic terms, where practicality comes to refer especially to increased efficiency, productivity, and profit.

All of this is neither good nor bad. But what does it do to the American mind to reduce its native pragmatism to only two questions: "Does it work?" and "What's in it for me?"

Is Hindsight 20/20?

LAWYERS TEND to be pretty self-critical. We might not readily show our self-doubt to others, or reveal how we second and third guess ourselves, but my sense is that we lawyers are very attuned to our own performance, and we are hard to please.

One way we go about this criticism is by going over and over things that have already happened. We get back from court, or read a deposition, or hang up the phone and then immediately replay the event, wondering if we should have said this instead of that. Perhaps the court rules against us, and off we go beating ourselves because if only we had made this argument better we would have won, and so on.

We follow a similar pattern, but with a completely different emotion, when we tell "war stories" or tales of success. These, of course, we do share with others. We highlight those especially brilliant moves that in our minds led to the success, and leave out everything else. But in both our self-critical and our self-congratulatory modes, we assume we now understand what happened in the past.

We have a saying for what I'm talking about: "Hindsight is always 20/20." The assumption is that when we look back on things that have already happened, we can see why and how they worked out as they did. Things that at the time were completely random or unpredictable occurrences are in retrospect seen as fitting into an overall story. Looking back allows us the big picture, and hindsight sees the intricate causal connections that inevitably lead to the now-known result.

But when does something qualify as hindsight? I might replay an event in my past a dozen, a hundred, a thousand times over the course of my life. How many times, for example, have you thought about that particular thing that happened when you were a kid? Depending on how old you are, you've probably looked at it through the eyes of twenty years, and thirty, and sixty. And who knows how long you will be able to go back and visit again? Older people tell me the older you get the more you return to the old places.

So, say you're fifty and you're going over, again, something that happened when you were thirty. It seems to me that your earlier attempts at hindsight are now part of the event being remembered, and so they must be included in the current attempt at hindsight. In other words, hindsight has to look at and through its own former manifestations, which means that hindsight itself is altering, perhaps continuing, the experience being viewed. This is similar to the recognition in the natural sciences that the experimenter cannot really be separated from the experiment, and that the very fact of viewing an event through an experimental eye necessarily influences what is seen.

Another problem with this 20/20 hindsight idea is that the events we see in hindsight seem to change over time. Hindsight seems to get clearer as our experience allows for deeper and deeper insights. What we thought we saw clearly at age twenty we now at age forty think we *really* see clearly. But by the time we're eighty who knows what we'll think? Remember, the only way we could ever know whether our hindsight really gets clearer with age would be through hindsight itself, which means we never get old enough to know for sure.

If hindsight is so perfect, after all, why are there so many history books about the same events? How many biographies of Lincoln do we need if hindsight is indeed 20/20?

The fact is that hindsight is a fictional activity. It presents itself as being 20/20, yes, but that is simply how it presents itself. Maybe hindsight even believes it is 20/20, but that's different from being 20/20. Hindsight certainly is something we do all of the time, and by claiming it fictional I don't mean to diminish its enormous value one whit. Rather, recognizing the fictional dimension of looking back actually enhances its vision. Once freed from the artificial restraints of having to see the big picture, hindsight can enable us to see the many stories in every event. Hindsight can teach humility—not only by offering proof that we didn't know what was going on then, but by assuring us we don't know what's going on *now.* The events of life can rarely be seen clearly, and even when they seem clear there are almost always other equally clear visions of the same events.

The *psyche,* or soul, loves to go back over things, but it doesn't do so with an idea of reaching final answers. Soul remembers for the sake of deepening one's sense of experience itself. From this perspective, looking back can also be imagined as looking at the back of things, taking a peek behind the scenes. It focuses on things unseen at the time even if we now see that they were in plain view all along. Hindsight at once sees the limitations of our vision while providing evidence that there are a thousand ways to see anything. And, if we are honest with ourselves when we get in our self-congratulatory mode, we will admit that, in hindsight, we have no more idea why things go right than why they go wrong.

Psychological reflection teaches very clearly that things are never clear. The experiences of a lifetime don't resolve themselves into definable segments in space and time, but rather persist throughout life. Their origins and boundaries remain obscure, their dynamics always a mystery, and their significance an open question at least until the end. To see such things, hindsight must be allowed to see in ways that allow it to see. It often takes a shaded eye to look back upon the random events and unexpected occurrences that mark our way, and to see in them the workings of invisible hands. Such things are never clear, but then it is said that no mortal can ever see a god clearly.

I Am Not a Customer. I Am a Man!

I AM WRITING this during the early months of the presidential campaign, a time that does not typically bring out the best in us. It does, though, bring out things that are common in us. What especially interests me are the ideas that underlie the debates, the ideas everyone seems to rely upon whatever their political stripe. Despite all of the argument and bipartisanship, there is more agreement among Americans than we think.

That Americans hold certain deep ideas in common is not a new observation. Tocqueville noted that although Americans pay little attention to philosophy, "they have a philosophical method common to the whole people." This suggests that America's ideas have always been directly lived more than thought; they are instinctive, habitual, the reflex in our knee-jerk reactions.

These commonly held ideas show up more in our actions and expectations than in what we say. In politics, for example, a debate over ideas quickly gets lost in the very fact of the debate—who's winning, who's down, etc. This step away from content toward controversy reflects a deeper American conviction in and fascination with adversarial competition. What is said doesn't matter as much as who is getting lanced. But more than the dog-eat-dog fantasies of social Darwinism, and indeed incorporating them, is America's current, almost universal, adherence to economic ideas. Economics has become *the* defining metaphor in the American mind, beyond even family, religion, walk of life, ethnicity, race, or gender. Without knowing we do so, we mimic economic's deeper ideas in our everyday actions and thought. Its logic becomes our logic, its assumptions our habits, its value judgments our ethical norms.

I'll give you an example that hit me right between the eyes. Several Sundays ago I was listening to *This Week With David Brinkley,* and Steve Forbes was being interviewed by the regular cast. Cokie Roberts asked Mr. Forbes to account for his massive spending on advertising in the early primary states, and he defended himself by saying he had done more "retail campaigning" than any of the other candidates. I immediately thought to myself: "Whoa—Donaldson's going to have a field day with that one." I could just hear Sam Donaldson charging that Mr. Forbes was a rich businessman who could only think in terms of buying and selling. "Retail campaigning" was so patently insulting that I just knew it was something Mr. Forbes hadn't meant to say in public. I wasn't surprised that such a phrase existed, but I was sure it was for use behind closed doors. Being a good American, and so always ready for a fight, I leaned forward to watch the sparks fly.

Absolutely nothing happened. Cokie and Sam and George took the phrase right in stride. (David wasn't there—I'll bet he would have said something.) One of them, I think it was Sam, even used the phrase himself! I remember thinking that Mr. Forbes sounded completely natural and open when he said "retail campaigning," but when Sam said it he sounded odd, as if it were the first time he'd ever said it. It sounded as if he was repeating it to hear himself say it, and maybe even to show that he, too, was "in" on how things worked. But the bottom line (see how easily economic ideas slip in?) was that nobody objected to the phrase. It was accepted without pause as legitimate rhetoric for political conversation.

We all know what Mr. Forbes meant. He was contrasting his use of mass media advertising, which presumably is "wholesale campaigning," with actually meeting citizens face-to-face at the retail level. No, wait. Not citizens—customers. From this perspective, citizens are customers, Mr. Forbes is the product, political campaigns are advertising, and the goal is to get the voter to spend his or her vote to buy the product. Bribing for votes becomes a redundancy because voting is bribery—currency given in return for favor. Never mind, just make the sale.

This doesn't surprise you, right? In fact, many of you are probably thinking how naive I sound, how behind the times. Politicians selling themselves like soap? Advertisers running campaigns? Old news, you say.

My point, though, is the depth of our acceptance of this very unusual way of imagining human beings. We have made a kind of metaphysics out of our economic fantasies. It's one thing to be seen as a customer through the eyes of the market place, it is another to assume that *everything* is a market place. The former recognizes that we play many roles in many different contexts; the latter is an ontological claim about the nature of things in general.

If I go into Sears to look at washing machines, I don't mind being looked at as a customer. I am, in fact, there to shop. But isn't there something off about taking my sometimes status as customer and elevating it over all of the other things I also am? I'm sorry, but I think for a candidate for President of the United States to think of politics as a sales pitch, and to consider me a customer first and a citizen only as an afterthought, perverts the very idea of America. Aristotle said, "Man is a political animal." He ascribed to humans the natural instinct to join together despite our differences and to form political groups. The ancients saw this as a noble thing, maybe even the defining thing that makes us human. What would we say nowadays? Maybe something like "humans are producing and consuming socio-economic units." Roll over, Aristotle.

Our habitual ideas have enormous influence over our lives. Such ideas shape how we imagine the very nature of our experiences. Habitual ideas do what the word "habit" says they do—they hold us in their grasp. At the same time we embrace them, we are also embraced by them, held under their sway, left dancing to their tunes.

What Registers, What Doesn't

I READ AN INTERVIEW the other day with Al Dunlap, a businessman whom, I assume from reading the interview, is well known for his ability to "restructure" companies into more profitable enterprises. Profitable, that is, in terms of the shareholders. Not so profitable for those sacrificed in the bargain.

Most of the interview was filled with the kind of inflationary self-congratulation you might expect from someone who actually *believes* he is a "self-made" man. This "self-made" fantasy, though a fond one for the American mind, is really more a comment on forgetfulness. No one is self-made, and to maintain otherwise points to a lacuna in the person's soul, an empty spot that either is incapable of recognizing those on whom one depends, or prefers to reject this knowledge in favor of grandiose self-importance. Pat Buchanan rails against immigrants, Clarence Thomas repudiates affirmative action, Wall Street condemns the poverty its ideas create, and so on.

But that isn't what I want to tell you. I'm not interested in Mr. Dunlap as an individual, but rather in the remarkable degree to which his views as stated in the interview reflect commonly held ideas. The interview read like a composite view of modern American business ethics, and it spoke in the now familiar rhetoric of predatory capitalism, complete with slavish obeisance to the shareholder:

> INTERVIEWER: Besides the shareholders, whom do you see as the stakeholders in a company?
>
> MR. DUNLAP: None . . .

INTERVIEWER: So the notion of community responsibility, loyal employees who aren't shareholders, or long-term suppliers doesn't cut it?

MR. DUNLAP: Doesn't register. In our annual report you'll see we have one constituency. It's the shareholders. I don't believe in the stakeholder concept one minute. I believe in the fact that the shareholders take all the risks, the shareholders own the company. You work for the shareholder. They're the constituency to whom you have to be responsive.

Well you certainly can't fault Mr. Dunlap for being ambiguous, but certain ideas here are worth a closer look, whether or not you agree with his views. In fact, the first thing that jumps out at me is the overall tone of certainty and facticity with which his views are stated. From the perspective Mr. Dunlap represents, there simply is no question about any of this. Shareholders are not just the primary "constituency" of a business but the *only* constituency. We might disagree over how to maximize shareholder profit, but surely we agree that is what we are supposed, indeed obligated, to do. This principle is not open to debate, just as it is nonsensical from this perspective to imagine "maximized profits" in any terms other than actual cash in the pocket.

This certainty leads to complications. For example, if we take Mr. Dunlap literally, which is how he is speaking, then exactly what is a company obligated to do in the name of maximizing shareholder profit? What if the top executives of a company decide, for example, on the basis of a cost-benefit analysis, that the shareholders could make more profit if the company violated the clean air laws? Even taking into account getting caught and fined, let's say a bottom line benefit would inure to the shareholders. Is the company, under Mr. Dunlap's view, not obligated to break those laws? The clean air laws, remember, derive from a constituency that Mr. Dunlap's view doesn't recognize. Surely their authority cannot be allowed to take precedence over that of the shareholder's inalienable right to maximum personal gain. And so what if a few executives have to go to jail? Isn't that a price this view requires one be willing to pay?

Another observation. Not only is Mr. Dunlap's view absolutely certain of its correctness, it is incapable of even considering alternatives. Remember, it wasn't that Mr. Dunlap held this or that view about community responsibility, employee loyalty, and long-term suppliers, but that he didn't think about them at all. No, not "didn't," but couldn't. "Doesn't register," he said.

Please note that "doesn't register" is as much a comment on the capacities of the measuring instrument as on the phenomenon being registered. Just because community responsibility, employee loyalty, and long-term suppliers are off Mr. Dunlap's scope doesn't mean they are non-entities. Indeed for centuries they have been considered critical aspects of business, and, I suspect, still are in many quarters. It may be that Mr. Dunlap and others cannot see these things, but that is because the field of view imposed by their monocular perspective is too narrow. What is depressing is the stubborn stupidity of such a view. Not even the blind deny the fact of the visible world.

We all know to be suspicious when belief states itself as fact. In saner moments we all know that life is not so certain, and that nothing important is as clear as Mr. Dunlap's rhetoric implies. It may be clear to him, yes, but that is a statement of personal ideology, not metaphysics.

We might ask who within us likes such talk. Who likes to believe in such certainties? Who wants to be absolutely sure about things? Who can't stand being questioned in ways that upset standing beliefs? Who has trouble considering alternative viewpoints? Who dismisses dissenting voices as unrealistic and naive?

There was a mythical figure in antiquity named Kronos who ascended to absolute authority over the gods by castrating his father, who had been in charge, with a sickle. Thereafter, Kronos ruled with an iron hand, but remained worried that he, too, might someday be deposed by his own son. His solution to this problem was to eat his children as they were born, but his wife finally was able to save a son by giving Kronos a bunch of rocks in swaddling, which he downed without a thought. The son saved by this ruse was Zeus, who later deposed Kronos by castrating him just as Kronos had his father.

Nice and clean, don't you think? Very efficient. Tit for tat.

I wonder if Mr. Dunlap knows that story?

And Now, A Word for the Sponsors

PEOPLE SEEM to be having a lot of trouble these days despite being told by the handlers of The Market that they aren't. We are told that crime rates have dropped, but people still are feeling more and more afraid. We are assured that the economy is strong and growing, but people still are feeling more insecure and vulnerable. Politicians, pundits, and portfolio managers wonder how this can be. Why can't people see what's really going on and adjust their attitudes accordingly? Surely it must be psychological, maybe President Carter's "malaise," or President Clinton's "funk."

I have an alternative answer. I say people are right in their feelings, and that having such feelings in the face of contradictory evidence is itself a symptom pointing to deeper contradictions embedded in our everyday lives. Item: companies lay off workers and stock values rise. Item: unemployment goes down, Wall Street takes a tumble. Item: although studies show that "downsizing" is about as effective as tossing a coin, management across the nation has taken to it with mindless zeal. Item: although people are already afraid of the level of invisible toxins in everyday life, Congress tries to repeal environmental regulations. (Does anyone seriously believe that the planet would be cleaner a year from now if all environmental regulations were dropped?) Item: over 90 percent of Americans claim to be religious—do you see much evidence of this? Item: people preach global this and global that while most of us hardly know our next door neighbor's name. Item: people surf the Web looking for like-minded relationships while the actual, full-sentenced, embodied relationship becomes an endangered species. Contradiction and misdirection seem to me to be the order of the day in public life. So why should we be surprised when the American people begin to internalize these contradictions into their general world-view?

I have more evidence. The other day I drove up to see some friends of mine. I was driving on a stretch of interstate highway that I've never been on before, and I was doing about 70, just cruising along real nice. The speed limit was 65 mph, so of course I was in the far right-hand lane so I wouldn't get run over. Anyway, I'm zooming along when I see this huge shopping mall up ahead on the left side of the road. Now mind you there were at least four or five lanes of traffic, a few broad medians, an access road, and a parking lot between me and the mall, but this place was HUGE. I think it was three or four stories tall, and the entire front was covered in glass so you could see the signs for all of the stores inside.

I recognized the names of several popular chain stores, and there were a number of others I'd never heard of before. The names of the stores were all done in big red neon signs with a uniform style of lettering, like labels. I was checking out the stores when I realized that because of how the parking lot and all was laid out, people walking up to the mall couldn't see the signs on the upper stories at all. Only people on the highway could see those stores, which was why the signs were so big and bright and easy to read. Then it hit me: all of this was designed so that I could window shop while doing 70.

Another piece of evidence. My wife and I were watching television when a commercial came on for an "extended relief pain killer." The commercial started out saying that Americans get lots of headaches. It showed a group of people (perfect demographics, don't you know), while the announcer said in a voice-over that "everyone gets their own kind of headache" (American individualism even extending to the headaches we get). Then the commercial cut to showing one woman at work.

She was at her desk shuffling papers around and answering the phone and generally being very, very busy. She had kind of a frantic look on her face. Meanwhile, we heard her talking, saying that her headaches came on at work because of all the stress, but that with this new extended relief pain killer all she had to do was take one pill in the morning and it "lasted all day." What a deal.

Needless to say, I have a problem with all of this. I mean, come on. They're actually using this kind of frenzied work ethic crap to sell pills to cover up the fact that the way we work is making us sick. And we're buying it, along with just about everything else. God forbid we should try to change our way of doing business. God forbid we might take all of these headaches we're getting as a sign that there is something painful in how we have allowed the pace and content of our lives to outstrip our natural tolerances. Instead, don't question, don't resist these ridiculous styles of work; all you need is a pill that lasts all day. I have a new ad campaign for that company: Don't Militate, Medicate.

But even more insidious than the implications of such pieces of evidence is the degree to which we have mistaken our rightful outrage and feelings of oppression for psychological symptoms having to do with us. So let me be clear. I hate that commercial, and all that it stands for, not because of my father complex, or my problems with authority, or my repressed inner child, or any of the other sleight-of-hand diversions dished up by modern psychology. I hate that commercial because it is hateful. The outrage I feel at a passive/aggressive society that allows itself to be cowed by superficial and sordid economic theories is not a reflection of my problem, but of society's problem. If I sound insistent, I mean to. We have been mesmerized by a gold-plated watch, and unless we come to our senses our pain will continue and will worsen. But maybe that's okay with everyone. Especially now that we have a pill that lasts all day.

How It Happens

HERE is how it happens.

My wife and I were on vacation recently and we stayed in a rental house managed by a company that handled the rentals, routine cleaning, maintenance problems, etc., for the owners, who usually were from elsewhere. The second night we were there, we put a rental movie tape into the VCR, pushed the play button, and nothing happened. The VCR was busted. A mild disappointment because we like to watch movies, but no big deal.

The next morning, I called up the management office thinking they might have a spare VCR, or could help us get this one fixed. A lady answered, and after I told her my problem she said:

"We are not responsible for such items. If you'll look at the back of your rental contract you'll see that we are not responsible. All I can do is notify the owner."

Now let's pause right here. What has happened? My wife and I are on vacation at the beach. Slightly sunburned, muscles that have been tight for months beginning to relax, sighs of pleasure and spontaneous "ahs" coming with every new release. We like to watch movies, and our VCR doesn't work. On our coffee table lays a packet of materials the management office gave to us when we checked in, and from where I stand at the phone I can see big lettered mottos like "We never rest on your vacation," and, in even bigger letters, "Call us!" And now, having called with an admittedly minor request, I'm being told to look at the back of my contract?

So what do you think I did?

I got mad, naturally. Suddenly I wasn't on vacation anymore. Contract talk is law talk, and the next words out of my lips weren't those of the mellow beach bum who had placed the call but the sharp and aggressive words of a lawyer. Not only had this woman, no longer a lady, been rude, but she was throwing a contract at me with the glibness of an amateur. I happen to know a few things about contracts, and so on. The chest swells, the temples warm, the eyes narrow—all of the adrenaline responses that every lawyer knows. All in the split second between her response and my anger.

The ensuing argument quickly escalated. Voices became tighter, louder. And then, just as suddenly, a small voice told me "This is how it happens." It stopped me. I realized I was no longer interested in fixing the VCR, but rather in 1) winning the fight, and 2) affirming my lawyerly status. In fact, I realized only later how much these things seem to depend on one another in my lawyer mind.

I stopped in mid-thrust and tossed aside my sword. "Look," I said, "my wife and I are on vacation. We like to watch movies together. That's all. I had hoped you could help, but you can't."

Well, she got a bit flustered, rightly suspicious of some new maneuver on my part. She waited for the follow-up, but there was no follow-up. Then she explained, in a new voice, that most of the repair shops took a week or more to fix things, so that even if they took the VCR in that day they wouldn't be able to get it back in time for us to use. Like a cool sea breeze, she was talking to me.

I told her I appreciated her help, and went out to the beach. As I sat watching the waves I thought about what had happened. How brash her first response was. How ready I was to fight back. How the actual subject of our conversation, the broken VCR, became lost in our battle of wills. I remembered stories I've heard from matrimonial lawyers about how the most intense and intransigent fights seem often to attach to something silly, some object so obviously out of proportion with the fight over it that it almost seems chosen precisely for that reason, its ridiculousness crying out that what is happening is not connected to this world, or at least not to the world as we currently conceive it. When two people are ready to kill over a vacuum cleaner, we can be assured that the invisible world has come a-calling. I sat there thinking how stupid it all was. How stupid I was. How easily I had fallen into my legal habits. How much my lawyerly persona was tinged with red arrogance. That little voice I heard was right, this is how it happens. Wars, fistfights, trivial arguments with one's spouse, silly academic squabbles over turf and power, vicious political infighting for the sake of personal advancement. So many swords ready to flash, and in each contest the prize is lost: peace, integrity, intimacy, learning, a more just and beautiful world.

But then I thought more about that little voice. Who was it that knew what was happening? Obviously not me; I was otherwise engaged. In other times, this voice would have been more known to me. I would have had ideas to honor it, proper names to evoke it. For the old Greeks it was the *daimon,* one's tutelary spirit, the quiet cautionary voice to which Socrates attributed whatever wisdom he possessed. It is a voice of the soul, of course, now rarely listened for, and hardly audible over the Self's loud proclamations.

After this I dozed off, lost once again to sun and sea and romance. Hours later, when we went back to the room, we found the VCR sitting on the dinner table. Taped to the VCR was a handwritten, signed note by the lady I had talked to. She had picked up the VCR herself and taken it to a repair shop. It turned out to be easy to fix and now here it was, ready to go. She ended her note saying she hoped we had a wonderful vacation. And do you know what? We did.

A Declaration of Purpose

I HAVE WRITTEN about the law quite a bit over the last several years, and now and then find it useful to take stock. Much of what I have written has been an exercise in prolonged reflection on a particular idea—that the Law has its own psychological integrity that cannot be reduced to its practitioners or even to its history. I have rarely addressed the litany of problems that the modern mind likes to posit as reasons for its distress. I write little about "stress," much less "stress management," and rarely address how to "balance one's professional and private lives," or how to "cope" with such purportedly practical concerns as intemperate judges, pressuring clients, burgeoning case loads, and, of course, the intractable demands of the bottom line.

I resist such topics because, in my view, they divert us from more pressing concerns. They betray two enduring plagues of the modern soul: obsessive self-interest fueled by arrogant humanism, and the denigration of the mystery, wonder, tragedy, and constitutive beauty of life itself. The modern mind knows less about the life of the soul or *psyche* now than at any other time in history, and when faced with clearly psychological difficulties prefers to waste its time on managerial and administrative fixes that are, at best, stopgaps. We are all, each of us, daily buffeted by invisible presences, influences, memories, inexplicable urges that feel clearly to come from without. But the modern mind denies and ridicules these obvious realities because it does not understand them and because its simplistic theories and ideologies cannot encompass them.

Single-mindedness is inherently blind to the rest of life, and so remains locked securely within its tunnel vision.

So from the beginning I have espoused certain themes designed to irritate and disrupt our usual views of the law and its profession. One big theme has been that what we feel individually as symptoms are not wholly, and rarely only, individual problems. The soul is not a personal possession, and much of the soul's distress comes from without in the forms of caste-based organizations and amoral economic theories masquerading as jurisprudence, in bad lighting and uncomfortable furniture, in ascetic architecture that considers ornamentation a tool of parody, and, most important, in paltry ideas of insufficient beauty and power to properly serve the world and its inhabitants.

I rail like this because, to my mind, lawyers should be among the first to rebel against such oppression; we are, after all, trained to resist. But instead too many of my colleagues are converting to the modern fundamentalist ecumenical religion of maximizing material profit at all costs. We treat "subordinates" as little more than stubborn machines and see our colleagues as competitors for an ever-decreasing piece of the pie. And then, when the detritus of these destructive ideas begin to smother us, leaving us depressed or anxious, we go to therapy and talk about ourselves. We must awaken to the fact that the symptoms we feel lie mostly outside of us. It is the narcissism of the age that keeps us caught before the looking glass.

Another big theme has been that lawyers are different from non-lawyers. I do not mean that lawyers have personalities different from non-lawyers. Perhaps they do, perhaps they don't. I mean simply that lawyers are lawyers. Declaring oneself in such a fashion is an indication of devotion, and as lawyers we carry a particular responsibility as devotees of

Justice. We are supposed to exemplify her ways, to be careful in weighing our thoughts because they rest in her divine scale, slow with the sword, which in classical images of Justice is almost always held at her side, pointing downward toward the underworld and its slow-moving ways, not upright and erect, ready for use at the slightest provocation. All people enact mythical happenings, and so, too, lawyers are mythical figures in their own right, not only the flesh and blood mortals who are of course like all other mortals.

Many cultures have recognized that the calling to serve a particular god or goddess is what constitutes one's individuality. And so I have tried to emphasize a deeper respect for the natural burdens of serving a great and noble god. It is this service that interests me. It may well be that such service entails particular pains and sacrifices that cannot be ameliorated or "cured" but rather must be endured with dignity and appreciation. Surely this view is supported by the weight of evidence from religious traditions around the world.

An example of method. The modern lawyer says "I feel isolated." The modern therapeutic response is to try to make the lawyer feel more included. I have made this mistake myself. Often, in fact. But now I have come to think that perhaps the lawyer's feeling of isolation is doing what all symptoms do by expressing in distressed form what is really required. Is isolation somehow necessary to being a lawyer? Is there a divine purpose for this isolation? Could it be an attempt to protect Justice from the sordid economic theories and ideological rants that currently drive us? Perhaps what we feel as isolation is the Law's call for retreat, for quiet reflection in solitude, for the need to be alone with an idea. Perhaps if we tended more to reflection, the isolation would not return in such twisted form. And so on.

But more than anything else, I have wanted to encourage

people in complementing their normal habits of mind with the gifts of renewed imagination. Every life and every occupation can be dedicated to the freedom inherent in the life of the soul. Far from being excluded from this opportunity, it is my vision that the Law and its devotees are charged with the sacred duty of protecting for all the soul's right to live in accord with its chosen destiny.

Saving Icarus

MY PERCEPTION is that American life in general has become too fast. I get the feeling that many people, maybe most, have a sense of trying to keep up with a programmatic style of life that is tiring us out, making us cranky, and leading us to mistakes in judgment. Almost everyone I know talks about not having enough time to do something they would like to do. Usually, and this is significant, the things left out fall into the category of ordinary life—spending time with family, finding some time alone, going for a walk, or sitting with friends for a leisurely meal. We somehow find ourselves in a situation where the invisible things running our lives are out of step with the actualities of human experience.

Lawyers are no different in this regard. Surveys indicate that well over half of lawyers feel they don't have enough time for ordinary life. One would expect such feelings to have psychological ramifications for lawyers, and they do. Many of the symptoms that hound lawyers—depression, anxiety, obsessive behavior, a compulsive drive for success—arise in part from this deprivation of everyday experience. It's difficult to feel grounded in a world you are either racing through or climbing ladders to get above.

This manic rush also hurts the law. What happens to the law when half its practitioners lose contact with the mundane? If, as our tradition teaches, much of the law is common, and arises from the facts of daily life, then what happens to the law when its practitioners lose precisely this grounding? There are many possibilities. Perhaps the law gets overly concerned with abstractions, or begins to have trouble connecting with the society it seeks to serve. Perhaps this lack of actual grounding comes back through misplaced materialism. Perhaps the law becomes elite, talking increasingly to itself, looking down on the hoi polloi. Perhaps the law begins to act in ways that seem unusual to everyone else.

The main danger, though, is that mania contributes to (causes?) the loss of everyday pleasures. One clear indicator of the hold mania has on us is the degree to which all suggestions contrary to its wishes sound unthinkable to us. A monomaniacal complex requires all things to bend to its particular image, and often the only thing a person can see from outside such a complex is its single-mindedness. So some of the best places to look for clues to where we are caught by our modern mania is where we are intolerant.

An example. I once gave a talk to the partners of a large law firm. The general consensus was that things were going well financially for the firm, but that there was a general disease arising from the sheer pace and volume of everyday practice. There simply never seemed to be enough time.

I asked them why they didn't just work less. They were in charge of the firm; if they wanted to drop the yearly hours expected by the firm, then all they had to do was say so. One man immediately said that was impossible because of the overhead in the firm. Although I didn't see it at the time, I now see that this defensive move bespeaks a very unsettled soul. If you live life to satisfy something hanging over your head, then you will live a subservient and nervous life, a life especially hard on the spirit of the lawyer. At the time, though, I asked the man if they could tame the overhead if everyone in the room took a reduction in pay. I admitted to him that I didn't know what I was talking about in terms of finances, but that I did know to be suspicious of mandated structures that demand unnatural and hurtful commitments from us. He looked at me with a mixture of incomprehension and red-faced rage; I think he actually hated me. At the time I was surprised by the fervor of his reaction to such a simple question. Now I see that it was the red face of mania that I was looking into, a mania that understands nothing but wanting more, and hates anything that would curtail its drive to get it. How much I hurt for that man's soul. How horrible to be trapped in a mind hell-bent on self-destruction.

The curious thing is that the mania is probably doing us a favor. In my view, the mania points to deep, unfulfilled, and increasingly endangered needs in the soul. The soul must imagine freely. It must be allowed its own place and pace. Heraclitus said that "the soul has its own principle of increase," but modern mania outstrips the soul's pace, insisting it keep up with mania's double-time drum. Not even psychology, whose very name means "telling of the soul," uses the word *soul* anymore. So much of modern life works unconsciously against the soul simply because the soul and its values have been defined out by the modern mind. The modern view allows only the tired dualism of matter and spirit, *mater* and *pneuma,* body and mind—but no soul, no *psyche,* no reflective third place. Thus the cultural soul is trapped just like the soul in that red-faced man.

Psychologist C. G. Jung said that in the modern age, "the Gods have become diseases." If so, then maybe mania is leading us to a collapse that must come before soul can once again become viable. Myth says that Icarus had to fly too close to the sun; that destiny required his waxen wings to melt and him to fall. Perhaps that is where we are, enacting a necessary sacrifice of our high-flying selves. If so, then there is nothing to be done for that man in the audience or for our cultural soul; it simply is our lot to reach, to burn, to fall. But let us remember that this fate, too, has great value. We still tell the story of Icarus.

A Strange Idea

I CAME ACROSS a strange idea the other day. In fact, it might be only part of an idea, like an interesting piece of metal that you pick up on a walk and carry along with you, turning it over in your fingers.

The idea has to do with our need to make money. Some of the things I do, I do to make money, and if I didn't need to make money, I wouldn't do those things. I suspect this is true for most people, and that if most people suddenly became wealthy they would stop doing some of the things they are currently doing.

That means that the need for money keeps us doing things that we would not otherwise do. And here is the curious idea—what if this is immensely valuable and necessary? If you didn't need money, you would not do some of the things you now do, which means those things would lose your contribution and not be done the same way that you do them. Perhaps our need for money is like family in that it holds us to places, people, and chores we might otherwise refuse if given free choice.

Could it be that the world needs things done that go against our personal wishes, and so finds ways to ensure that those things get done? Could our need for money be such a way? Somehow I think it is important for us to do things we don't want to do. Otherwise our personal wishes alone come to determine our spheres of influence. But what if the world wants and needs things from us that are not commensurate with what we want or need? We might have talents we would just as soon not use, but the world needs them nonetheless, and so we must oblige. Not so we will be fulfilled in some way, but simply because things need to be done and we're handy.

Believe me that such ideas go against my grain. I prefer my long-held belief that people should be able to do pretty much anything they want to do. But that belief, I now see, cannot be taken too literally. Free, yes, but always within the larger context of the world and its needs. In other words, chores don't necessarily make us less free if they are necessary chores.

What would happen in a society of independently wealthy people? Try to imagine a society in which everyone is rich and there are no outside labor forces. Who would pick up the garbage? Who would write the laws? What would be the difference? What if life simply requires that certain things be done and that whoever is around must share the burdens of this daily maintenance? Being able to do whatever you want is therefore not a perquisite of independent wealth but its greatest danger, both a trapping and a trap. To appease only one's interests leads to virtual reality instead of real virtue, and replaces actual relationship and community with the passing ephemera of personal whim. The need for money, strange as it may sound, might actually make us more free by holding us to the hard tasks of maintaining a free world instead of losing ourselves forever in the prison of what we want.

So, when someone says, "I only work because I have to pay bills," we could hear both a lament pointing to an oppressive economic system, and also a testament to the world's need for that person's participation. After all, if a person only practices law to pay the bills, then those bills keep that person practicing law. Is it possible that this is a good thing regardless of that person's preferences? How many advances have been made in human civilization by people doing things that they didn't necessarily want to do?

To be clear, this isn't the old "hard times build good character" line. I'm saying that there are actually needs in the world that cannot be reduced to those darlings of therapy and capitalism, self-esteem and self-satisfaction. I'm saying that a boat doesn't really care whether cleaning the bilge builds your character—it just wants its bilge cleaned. How would our lives change if we honored, instead of fought with, the simple fact that the world requires things of us that we don't always want to do? Instead of feeling anxious and petulant because we are not fulfilling the impossible demands of personal freedom, we might actually relax a little, get the cleaner and brushes, and make the best of a bad situation.

I heard a story once, perhaps apocryphal, about a garbage man who won a large amount of money in a lottery. He immediately made a major change in his life by quitting his second job, but he kept on picking up garbage. When I heard this story, my first thought was that the guy had to be crazy. I mean, if I won the lottery, I'd be on a beach somewhere . . . and so on. And then my all-American, self-actualizing mind kicked in and I thought, no, perhaps he likes being a garbage man, and is satisfied and happy with what he is doing. Perhaps it is my knee-jerk ridicule that is crazy, not this happy man who chooses to do a difficult job.

But now this strange idea we've been talking about suggests another possibility. Perhaps he keeps collecting garbage not because he wants to but because he doesn't want to. Perhaps he doesn't particularly like being a garbage man, but feels it incumbent on him, *especially now that he is wealthy,* to continue. Perhaps he does it because it needs to be done, and figures such a difficult job might as well be done by someone without money worries to add to the back-breaking effort already required. Perhaps he is not a happy garbage man, but a Sage illuminated by Fortune.

Somebody Sound the Alarm

TWO EXAMPLES of a world in need of attention.

I was on an airplane the other day and was flipping through the airline's magazine when I came upon a column about style in the workplace. One question concerned the increased practice in corporate circles of "casual days" when workers are encouraged to come to work "dressed down." The questioner wanted to know how a CEO was supposed to dress on these days in order to distinguish himself (the questioner's word) from the people who worked for him.

I was excited by this question because it so neatly summarized something I hate. It replaced style with the usual, hoary economic elitism that permeates so much of our modern views of the human, as if a person's worth is determined by job title and earning capacity. It also showed how this elitism usually brings other forms of bigotry along with it, as witnessed by the questioner's assumption that only men can be CEOs. I couldn't wait for the columnist to teach this questioner a lesson, and I got my wish. According to the columnist, the CEO should wear an expensive cashmere sport coat, imported trousers, etc. He should always dress more expensively than the people who work for him, and even on casual days should affect an air of distant stature. Accessories, too, could help to set this higher being apart—a special pen,watch, cufflinks (on casual day!) or other expensive baubles could help do the trick.

If I'd had a parachute I would have jumped. I was beside

myself with anger at the denigration of style that this exchange revealed. Here were two people who knew nothing about style. No challenge arose as to why the CEO should wear certain clothes to distinguish himself when one purpose of casual days presumably was to help blur such lines. No case was made that the CEO's style, if he was truly a leader, would naturally stand out in the eyes and minds of his employees no matter how he dressed. No attempt was made to show the questioner how ugly and unstylish his caste mentality was, or how such ideas would forever keep him from his own style. And no mention was made of how impossible it must be to be casual in the company of people who think they are better than others because they own a $400 pen.

A person with style has it no matter how they are dressed or what they own. All of us could give examples of people who have enormous style despite their "lower" place on the economic ladder. And we know the other side, too, the people of wealth and excess who have the latest and most expensive of everything and yet are lumpish and unattractive in their manners and mannerisms. Surely style comes from elsewhere than a cashmere coat, and reveals itself in mysterious ways not subject to a person's bank account. Economics might be a way of keeping score in the numbers game of predatory capitalism, but it is a poor judge of style.

My second example comes from a television commercial that you perhaps have seen. A middle-aged man is washing his car with his twenty-something daughter watching.

"How's the new job," he asks.

"Fine," she says.

"Still getting those headaches?"

"Yes. My doctor said it's stress."

"Did he give you anything?" asks dear old Dad.

"Brand X [over-the-counter] extended relief."

Alarmed, Dad asks, "Nothing stronger?"

If we follow the narrative of this heart-warming scene, we have a young woman whose job is making her sick. So sick, in fact, that she had to go to an obliging doctor to be medicated. Her father's concern, however, *her father,* is whether her medication is strong enough.

If Dan Quayle can pick on Murphy Brown to argue for a return to his view of family values, I can pick on this fictional pair to show how pathetic our attitudes about life and work have become. Talk about child abuse! Her father might have objected to the fact that his daughter was doing something that was making her sick. God knows if she had said she smoked a little marijuana now and then the commercial would have ended with her brain frying in a skillet. But here is a clear message to do what you're told to do, without complaint, even if it is hurtful or wrong. The important thing is to keep the economic engine running at full speed (precisely the mechanistic view that leads to stress and hyperactivity) while keeping your suffering from impeding progress. This is the propaganda we are feeding our children and swallowing ourselves; and we wonder why Ritalin and Prozac, and the suffering they imply, have become commonplace.

These examples point to mean-spirited and hurtful views of human life that have nothing to do with what happened to me as a child, or my self-esteem, or whatever other hand-wringing theories psychology espouses nowadays to keep us from addressing the facts as we find them. Introspection, when your house is on fire, only ensures that you will not make it out alive. What we need is to fight the fire. But until we find the courage to snuff out the ugliness that is engulfing our world, the soul and all it contains will continue to suffer.

Somebody sound the alarm.

A Coarse Campaign

MY TOWN had village elections not too long ago, and a few weeks before election day I received a campaign flier for one of the parties running a slate of candidates. It began with the declaration that "the most important thing in any community is property values." It then asserted that property values had declined in my neighborhood over the past few years, and described how certain public places in my town had fallen into disrepair. This neglect, according to the flier, could be seen in the peeling paint on our water tower, unkempt storefronts, and the like. The flier argued that unless my town rectified such blights it would be unable to attract the "right kind" of residents to move into town.

I made up my mind then and there to vote for anybody but this gang. The claim that the most important thing in a community is property values is both wrong and crass, and, having grown up in the South during the civil rights movement and lived in Chicago for over fifteen years, I have heard this "right kind of person" language before. Translated, and here I am being kind, it means "people just like me."

Within a week came an answering flier from the opposing party. I was ready to read a double-barreled refutation of the first flier's outlandish claims. Things started off well with a bold-faced statement that the previous flier had been wrong. But then the bottom dropped out of my spirits when I read that the reason the first flier was wrong was that property values had gone up, not down.

No other challenges were made.

Nowhere was the core claim that property values are the most important thing in a community shown to be sad, selfish, and distinctively non-communal. None of these purported community leaders spoke of decency, a welcoming attitude to newcomers, mutual support of the elderly who make up a sizable portion of my town, or consideration among neighbors. Nowhere was the pig-eyed desire to be surrounded by the "right kind" of people exposed for what it is. The message, as if we don't hear this enough, was that value means money and nothing more. If you want more money, vote for me. What else is there to say?

Everything goes downhill once actual values are deflated to hard currency. From my perspective, a town that equates its worth and attractiveness with property values is deplete of both. Imagine a place that doesn't paint its water tower to make it more beautiful, or as a testament to communal affections, or even to satisfy obligations of maintenance and care, but only so property values won't go down. Imagine a place that doesn't maintain its common spaces in order to attract and propitiate the spirits and gods that are necessary to every community, but only so it can attract the right kind of people—the same kind of people, mind you, who have let the water tower go wanting. I say these are paltry ways of imagining community.

This unquestioning appeal to property values is a further example of the introversion and degradation of public life brought about in our time by a generation devoted only to getting as much as possible for their personal, private use. I must get mine, says this view, and screw everybody else. And, because we get the leaders we deserve, we end up with politicians unwilling to proclaim the nakedness of such views.

Instead we get coarse campaigns directed to our selfishness and fears, with arguments centering on whether the bottom line is up or down.

I have never found the cost of someone's house to determine whether they are good or bad neighbors. I have found people with much less than I to be attentive and caring, and those with much more than I to be boorish and uncaring, and vice versa. I am quite confident when I say that neighborliness is not a function of the size of one's bankroll, and that community cannot be reduced to property values.

I feel bad for my town to have people talk about it this way. I feel sorry for the old water tower when it is cheapened by rhetoric reducing it to a symbol for advancing personal status. I am saddened that any town should be so lacking in actual values that all it has left to talk about is the value of its parcels, no longer living places of natural beauty but dead entries on a ledger. I am saddened when community maintenance, which in other contexts is a laying on of loving hands, becomes a kind of standing advertisement, not for a community, but for a product offered for sale. And I am sickened that after all these years I still must hear talk about the right kind of people when it is the people who talk this way who make living ugly and abusive.

I know that I must take responsibility for the meager discourse that weakens my town. All I know to do is to resist such talk with whatever talents I might possess. But I am not a leader, and so I ask those of you who are to heed my simple plea—do not give us what we want when we traffic in ugliness. Do not use your energies and gifts to lead us into temptation but to deliver us from evil.

Law and the Enduring Heart of Culture

I HAVE A DREAM. In my dream we live in a time where the sordid ideas that have run us ragged lo these many years have finally collapsed under the weight of their own pretensions. Having finally maxed out in our manic attempts to maximize productivity, we have crawled away from our crash bruised but curiously refreshed, our eyes reopened to the world as something wondrous instead of something there for the taking. Darwinism, with its simplistic ideas of survival and competition, has given way to ideas worthy of our fellow inhabitants, the animals and plants and things of the world. Dualism, with its silly division of body and mind, has retired and gone home to wonder how it could have been so wrong. Secular claims of human superiority have fallen humble before the mysteries that they tried so long to ignore. And the soul's captivity in the human mind has ended, releasing both soul and mind into a world once again seen as alive without need of our projections.

In my dream, people have learned the value of good manners, assuming that all people are worthy of such fair treatment. Workers look forward to their day's work, knowing in their hearts that they are valued and their talents respected. They work to do the best they can, not to satisfy a Boss, but to do right by the work itself, dedicated to the beauty inherent in every task. Lovers strive to create places of intimacy for their partners, not so they might get the same in return, but because such selfless giving comes naturally to those in love. And our leaders are led by noble ideals, encouraging us to follow them even as they learn from our support and trust.

Beauty abounds, returned to its indispensable place in the nature of things. Love, freed from meager ideas of sentimentality and self-interest, is seen everywhere, his arrows striking us with honeyed elegance, causing our wings to grow and our spirits to take flight. Decency is no longer mistaken for weakness, and human interactions are no longer debased to chest-pounding shows of strength and superiority. There is little talk of power, and no need for talk of empowerment.

In my dream, bigotry based on gender, race, ethnicity, or religion no longer holds the court of daily discourse, and multiculturalism has become an archaic term. Difference is simply assumed and celebrated, each person taken as an each, replete with his or her own integrity and without need of prepackaged identities or store-bought esteem. People wait to see who someone is, and each person is encouraged to show his or her own special bloom.

Children in my dream say please and thank you, having learned this simple grace from their elders, and there is little need for our current fixation on the child. Instead, adults are adults, and children learn all they will ever need to know by this easy example.

There is still ugliness, but we refuse to fuel its fires, having learned instead to embrace it with maturity and compassion. Prisons still exist, yes, but they are places of learning and cultivation, no longer sweaty pits of hatred and depravation.

In my dream, the old are welcomed to be old, free from delusions of eternal youth. Elders move slowly among us, teaching us the importance of slowness and the value of long perspective. We ask their advice and are proud to heed it, no longer shackled by the insane notion that only the new can be right.

In my dream, our beautiful America has learned that we must show the rest of the world we are willing to bear the burdens of doing what is right and just instead of only what is expedient to our so-called national interest. Our weapons lie dormant and unthreatening, and the miracles of our technology are clearly dedicated to nurturing, not abusing, our fragile planet. Instead of demanding others to sacrifice so we might add to our convenience, it is our gold that is the first to be offered. And when we meet at the table of compromise with our worldly companions our hands are clean, ready to reach out to help others less fortunate to ascend the steps of liberty.

And in my dream lawyers, those wayward darlings of the soul, have returned home to the temple of Justice after their detour into the crass and harsh domains of greed and personal advancement. They shine with Her light, and are living examples of the Law in a world that has come to welcome their example. Law firms are exemplars of kindness and compassion, dedicated to serving the soul of the Law, and the hearts of their employees are no longer heavy with fear and insecurity but burst forth with an incredible lightness of being.

In my dream we have learned that there can be no culture without Law, and the Law has reclaimed its place in the heart of every man and every woman, each person called to do justice in their thoughts and deeds. Neighbors join together to attend to their neighborhoods, encouraged by the Law's blessings. Business people find that the world is not full of sharks after all, but that sharks are only one species in a sea of plenty. Resort to Law no longer means only a call to the police or a suit filed for revenge, but instead quickens with the glory of a promise made and kept and the trusting firmness of a handshake.

Perhaps I will awaken someday to find my dream a reality, perhaps not. But I will continue to work to accomplish its ends even as I slumber, one foot in this world and the other in my dream. You, too, can join me here if you wish, but first you must promise not to stir me with loud claims of how things really are. A dream is no place for such talk, and it is such a beautiful dream.

Conclusion

THROUGHOUT this book, an idea has struggled to make itself apparent, an idea so strange to the modern mind that it sounds almost nonsensical. That idea is this, that Law is in service to Beauty, and through Beauty pleases the many gods. From this perspective, the work of Law is the aesthetic arrangement of the world, and only through its dedication to this divine end may the Law become manifest in the world, apparent to the hearts of mortals, formative of culture and civilization.

One reason this idea sounds farfetched is that we have, for the most part, lost the idea of Beauty itself. In our world, Beauty has either been reduced to effete ideas of the pretty and cute, or inflated into predetermined ideals. The former leaves us wallowing in Hallmark sentimentality, while the latter tempts us toward fascism and bigotry—only this is beautiful and nothing else. But the Beauty of the ancients was not so circumscribed. For a mind versed in myth and imagination, Beauty is nothing less than the showing of things as they are, the shining through of the gods in the many things of the world. Socrates did not possess the visage of a leading man, yet Plato calls him beautiful because he was as he appeared.

Without Beauty, goes the old ways, things do not appear. The invisible pressures of justice, the strainings of the Law, the ideals that inspire the mind—without Beauty these all remain hidden from view, and we are left with a world without taste or style, all things drab and strangely lifeless. Only when Beauty arrives does the world become manifest, and we are able to sense the wonder and complexity of a world suddenly revealed.

In the ancient world, the word for order was *kosmos*, and this idea had little to do with regimentation and strictures. James Hillman puts the old idea thus:

> [*K*]*osmos* . . . was an aesthetic idea, and a polytheistic one. It referred to the right placing of the multiple things of the world, their ordered arrangement. Kosmos did not mean a collective, general, abstract whole. It did not mean universe, as turning around one point (*unus-verto*) or turned into one. This translation of cosmos into universe is a typical Roman imperialism unifying and obliterating the Greek particular sense of the world. . . . Kosmos also implied aesthetic qualities such as becomingly, decently, duly, honorably, creditably. "Cosmetics" is closer to the original meaning than is our word "cosmic" (as vast, unspecified, empty).

Hillman's words warrant long and repeated contemplation by those who claim to serve the Law in our world. Here is a notion of "order" worthy of the phrase "Law and Order." It takes little reflection to see how abstract and imperialistic, how "Roman" are our modern notions of Law, imbued as they are with the fictions of over-arching unified theories, single-minded answers, and stern control. How typical it is for us to think there can be only one "right" answer, only one sufficient explanation. And yet, even to our modern minds, the essence of the Law remains common, our law books filled with the slow deposits of particular cases, each unique, each deserving of a careful, dare I say beautiful, attention. A Law dedicated to Beauty does not get lost in starry-eyed idealisms or cosmic principles. Little time is wasted on grand theories of jurisprudence that matter only to others who, of course, offer their own competing grand theories. Law in service to Beauty remains among us, asking that we work with an aesthetic eye, refining and polishing, turning and shaping our responses to each situation, guided throughout by a vision that our work must be pleasing, that it must be beautiful.

Imagine if in our courts of law our decisions were guided by the hand of Beauty. Precedent would stand, not as a determinant, but as an example of how other artists have painted a similar scene. Clients would not be shrunken into narrow categories of self-interest, but would be more fully imagined in terms of their many connections to a world intimately imagined and carefully composed. Lawsuits would no longer be imagined as hand-to-hand combat, me against you, with winning or losing the only possible results, but rather as aesthetic challenges, asking that all involved strive to do justice to Beauty's abiding concerns. Each case would be seen as another opportunity to do something wonderful, and our success or failure would be judged by whether we have perceived what is there and responded appropriately.

For the soul, all things display themselves through beauty, each thing pleased to be just itself, its very being revealed in and through its precisely crafted image. And so the Law must take care in its abstracting habits, reminding itself that Beauty does not belong only to the reifying demands of Apollonic consciousness that prefers explanations over engagement. The things of this world do not appear as they do because of our ability to figure them out, and their integrity and display are not the results of our projections. Things are as they are, their natures apparent to a soul that trusts its innate talents for sensation and sensibility. But lose Beauty, and the senses fail; lose Beauty, and all is lost.

In the old tale of Apuleius, *Psyche,* or soul, was a lovely young woman who served in the temple of Aphrodite, the great goddess of Beauty. In ancient language, Psyche was a *therapeutes* in Aphrodite's temple, an attendant, a caring supplicant. To my mind this suggests that the task of therapy is a task dedicated to Beauty, and I have long pressed this claim on my fellow psychotherapists. Now I extend this claim to the carriers of Law in this world—which means each of us. Without Beauty justice remains disembodied, an invisible potential devoid of actuality. Only through Beauty does justice become manifest, so unless Law persistently encourages Beauty, its work will at best remain formless and abstract, and at worst will fall into ugliness.

The psychologist C. G. Jung once said the "image *is* psyche." This connection, even equation, of soul and imagination has a long and honorable tradition, even if in our time it has become a small and tenuous thread. But if the Law is to serve Beauty it must regain a fuller sense of imagination as the royal road to soul. The Law has plenty of intellect, plenty of smart people ready to test themselves against other smart people. What is needed, desperately, is a Law of sophisticated imagination. The world is revealed through images, which means that it is Beauty that inspires imagination, making it possible for us to sense the movements of soul and to appreciate its many expressions. Without imagination the smartest mind remains deaf and dumb, lacking taste and the pleasures of touch, its nose incapable of smelling the infinite bouquets of the world.

The intellectual mind is itself a style of imagining, though it prefers to pretend otherwise. Is this pretense why so many of the mind's creations today seem so dull and flat, mere explanations offered in the face of overwhelming mystery? Is this why the Law seems so often lost amidst a forest of technicalities, so locked within staid responses recited from a code or rule that was dead on arrival?

And so at the end of this little book I offer you a big idea. Let us reconsider the place of the Law in our world. Let us set aside tired and ponderous ideas of the Law as a bulwark against Chaos, of adversity and conflict as the harbingers of truth, and of Order as something a superior gives to underlings. Even if we currently do not have ideas to replace or complement our usual thoughts, let us have the courage to resist the ugliness that surrounds us. Let us put our faith in the soul, trusting that it means us no harm, and open our imaginations to the endless possibilities of divine service in the name of Beauty. If the world we leave behind is not more beautiful than the one to which we were born, if we have not moved closer to being able to sense the things under our very noses, if our imaginations have not become more sophisticated and complex, then what, really, have we accomplished? Security is no substitute for courage, tolerance not a replacement for respect, argument not the soul's manner of speech.

Soul, Beauty, and Love go together, and when one suffers all are implicated. So let us reopen the case of the Law, asking whether we missed something significant in our rush to judgment. It is never too late to appeal to the Gods, never too late to ask for their help. But we must show them that our hearts are open and our intentions just. May we be guided by a vision of a more beautiful and just world, and comforted by the old idea, only recently misplaced, that the Gods take care of those who serve them. Or at least so let us imagine.